CONNECTED TEACHING

# CONNECTED TEACHING

## Relationship, Power, and Mattering in Higher Education

*Harriet L. Schwartz*

Foreword by Laurent A. Parks Daloz

Afterword by Judith V. Jordan

STERLING, VIRGINIA

Published by Stylus Publishing, LLC.
22883 Quicksilver Drive
Sterling, Virginia 20166-2019

Library of Congress Cataloging-in-Publication Data
Names: Schwartz, Harriet L., author.
Title: Connected teaching : relationship, power, and mattering
    in higher education / Harriet L. Schwartz ; foreword by
    Laurent A. Daloz ; afterword by Judith V. Jordan.
Description: First edition. | Sterling, Virginia : Stylus Publishing,
    LLC., 2019. | Includes bibliographical references and index.
Identifiers: LCCN 2018046110 (print) | LCCN 2018059671
    (ebook) | ISBN 9781620366387 (ePub, mobi) | ISBN
    9781620366394 (uPDF) | ISBN 9781620366363 (cloth :
    acid-free paper) | ISBN 9781620366370 (paperback : acid-
    free paper) | ISBN 9781620366387 (library networkable
    e-edition) | ISBN 9781620366394 (consumer e-edition)
Subjects: LCSH: College teaching. | Teacher-student
    relationships. | Interaction analysis in education.
Classification: LCC LB2331 (ebook) | LCC LB2331 .S377
    2019 (print) | DDC 378.1/25--dc23
LC record available at https://lccn.loc.gov/2018046110

13-digit ISBN: 978-1-62036-636-3 (cloth)
13-digit ISBN: 978-1-62036-637-0 (paperback)
13-digit ISBN: 978-1-62036-638-7 (library networkable
e-edition)
13-digit ISBN: 978-1-62036-639-4 (consumer e-edition)

Printed in the United States of America

All first editions printed on acid-free paper
that meets the American National Standards Institute
Z39-48 Standard.

Bulk Purchases
Quantity discounts are available for use in workshops and
for staff development.
Call 1-800-232-0223

First Edition, 2019

*To Brenda, with love*

*And for my teachers, with deep and enduring gratitude*

# CONTENTS

Some years ago, on a kayaking retreat amidst the jagged coastlines and misty ancient forests of Southeast Alaska, alive with ravens and eagles overhead, a wolf pack howling in the forest, and salmon thrashing beneath us, we learned what a vital thing an estuary is. Everything happens there. It's the commons of the natural world; species diversity is greatest in this rich soup where the boundary of the sea and the land intersect and overlap, where life thrives. This is what Harriet L. Schwartz has given us in her wonderful book: a vision of an educational estuary where the complex lives of learners and teachers come together and are revealed.

As a fledgling student teacher decades earlier, I sat entranced in a large lecture hall as Lawrence Kohlberg elaborated his emerging theory of moral development. I had read my Dewey, and the idea that as teachers we ought to be doing more than merely imparting information fascinated me. But what was that *more*? How to do it? How could I get a handle on how students *grow* into smarter, wiser people? Beyond that, what *else* were they learning in school as they grew? How could I better understand the connection between education and growth so I might be a more conscious and effective presence in their lives?

Some years later, as a college teacher and budding scholar, I found myself in a workshop with William Perry, who had merged earlier work on authoritarianism with his own study of epistemological development in college students. When I walked out two days later, I had begun to grasp what would become the heart of my own understanding of adult development: an understanding elaborated and enriched over the years by a host of developmental scholars, including Fowler, Gilligan, Kegan, Belenky and colleagues, Mezirow, and Parks. Those years were downright thrilling. Dewey's promise was truly coming to fruition.

Meanwhile, just down the road from where much of this work was spawned, Jean Baker Miller had been writing about women at Wellesley's Stone Center, which subsequently became the nation's preeminent center for research and reflection on the centrality of *relationship* to learning and education. (In fact, despite the full wall of books about men's development that has mushroomed in my library, Miller's [1987] groundbreaking *Toward a New Psychology of Women* remains the single most insightful description of male psychology that I know).

In *Connected Teaching: Relationship, Power, and Mattering in Higher Education*, Schwartz moves the conversation about more fruitful teaching ahead in a magnificent way. By integrating developmental theory with the influential contributions of Relational-Cultural Theory, she further broadens our attention from the student in isolation to the recognition of the larger ecology within which students invariably learn and ultimately grow. Teaching, she reminds us over and over and in dozens of ways, is about *relationship*. She helps us to recognize the challenges of teaching that confront teachers who truly care about how as well as what their students learn, and about *who* they are—and who they long and need to become. And then she gets deliciously specific.

I have taught for over 50 years, and reading her detailed and gritty text, it all comes back: the thrill of a student who gets it, the disappointment with one who doesn't, the magic moment when a class glows with a fresh insight, the naïve expectations that we know must be disappointed, the painful skepticism in the back of the classroom, the wary eye from a frightened student, the tender and risky moment when we reveal about ourselves something a student needs to hear, the hard conversation, the joke that falls flat, the student who needs so much more than we can ever give, the joyful laughter when we all just celebrate being together.

On those rare occasions when we actually talk about our work with other teachers, it is not only the subjects we teach but also the stories of the students and their lives that captivate us. Yet even more refreshing is that while her account is packed with practical experience and wise reflection, Schwartz gives us a set of conceptual baskets that hold these insights and struggles and helps us sort them, to find a stance from which to make sense of it all and thus adjust our own teaching more productively.

With refreshing candor, Schwartz catalogues the hidden power differentials; students' anxiety and projections; the complexities of gender, race, or class; our own teacherly hubris; and the often excruciating conflicts among institutional demands, student needs, and society's expectations. With a sure hand born of well-crafted care and humbling tumbles, she offers a trove of conceptual tools—almost all new to me but enormously helpful—that include asymmetrical primacy, managing boundaries, context collapse, disruption (a good ecological term), confident transparency, resistance, failure, mattering, psychological contract. Looping around, connecting dots we'd never have thought related, and weaving fresh patterns of meaning, we find ourselves in the end, held in a marvelous fabric, a cloak, a robe.

Over and over, as I read, I found myself wishing I had another lifetime to teach with Schwartz's insights in hand. So I wish for the reader, privileged to practice one of life's most honorable and rewarding arts, to curl up with this nourishing and delightful read, to soak up its invigorating and practical wisdom, and then plunge back into those lush and complex waters where life flourishes. This is what we live for.

Laurent A. Parks Daloz
Senior Fellow
The Whidbey Institute
Cascadia Bioregion

## Reference

Miller, J. B. (1987). *Toward a new psychology of women*. Boston, MA: Beacon Press.

This book explores teaching as a relational practice—a practice wherein connection and disconnection with students, power (ours and theirs), identity, and emotion shape the teaching and learning endeavor. As such, I propose that understanding ourselves is as important as understanding the content of our disciplines. This self-awareness, coupled with our ability to connect with students, drives not only our effectiveness but also our resilience and well-being through the demands and the highs and lows of a life in education.

Relational-Cultural Theory (RCT) informs and inspires connected teaching. Connection—the experience of engaging in growth-fostering interactions and relationships—is essential to human development and well-being; this is the premise of RCT (Miller & Stiver, 1997). RCT's founding scholars proposed the theory would be relevant in not only therapeutic practice "but also workplaces, schools, and other institutions—in other words, all of life" (Miller & Stiver, 1997, p. 17). Nonetheless, RCT has been applied primarily in therapy and social work arenas. However, as you will see, RCT has much to offer those of us devoted to student learning and development, providing a theoretical foundation from which to understand the transformative potential of teaching as a relational practice.

Teaching from a relational perspective is neither soft nor simple, and so a few clarifications are in order. RCT views *relationship* not as a pleasant option in professional work but rather as vital to any educational endeavor. The idea is not to add likeability to one's teaching repertoire but to understand how relationship is central and essential in education. At the same time, RCT's focus on relationship should not confuse our thinking about the role of a teacher and our approach to interacting with students. Educators hold distinct responsibilities and commitments in our work with students—teaching and learning relationships differ from therapy, peer friendships, and other sorts of formal and informal human connections.

In addition, RCT does not view relationships as inherently or essentially light and easy. Instead, RCT recognizes relationships as dynamic and complex. RCT is about developing relational capacity and clarity and nuanced authenticity (Jordan, 2010); relational professionals bring a level of sophistication and informed transparency to their work and are skilled at engaging in good conflict (Miller, 1976) as well as the joyful moments of teaching and learning.

Along with RCT, the works of several writers help position this book. Connected teaching is not a step-by-step method. It is rooted in awareness of self and other, and is a way of being. Laurent A. Parks Daloz (1999) asserts that education "is not a bunch of tricks or even a bundle of knowledge. Education is something we neither 'give' nor 'do' to our students. Rather, it is a way we stand in relation to them" (p. xvii).

Daloz and several other epochal thinkers, including Parker Palmer, bell hooks, Stacey Waite, and Stephen Brookfield, have also shaped me as a learner of teaching. In distinct voice, each of these educators has written from experience while also drawing from the literature to shine new light on the teaching endeavor. Like the best songwriters, they share personal stories that are at once specific and universal. Their words strike a resonant chord, helping us interrogate and understand our own experiences as we travel through a career of working with students.

These gifted educators reflect on and describe the role of emotion in teaching. For example, hooks (1994) proclaims, "As a classroom community, our capacity to generate excitement is deeply affected by our interest in one another, in hearing one another's voices, in recognizing one another's presence. . . . To begin, the professor must genuinely value everyone's presence" (pp. 7–8).

Courageous, these writers also share their imperfections and vulnerability, helping us see our own struggles and failures as inevitable rather than weak. For example, Waite (2017) unveils failure as both painful and promising:

> We don't frequently write about our failures as teachers, about those moments our students show us to ourselves. . . . I want to stand for some time in the light of my own failure. I want to illuminate how pedagogical change might happen. (p. 72)

While stories and personal perspective inform connected teaching and this book in particular, I also draw heavily on empirical and established theoretical literature from both teaching and psychology, as well as leadership and organizational studies.

As I invite you to take this journey, I encourage you to pause and remember your best teachers. What do you recall about these educators? How did they enter the learning space? How did they relate to you, the course content, and the discipline? How have you tried to emulate your best teachers, and how have you taught in opposition to those you viewed negatively?

Likewise, which individual students and groups of students are most memorable? Are there difficult interactions that still burden you? Which students and interactions were energizing? And when have you known that you and your work as a teacher matter?

Next, I suggest you consider your biography. How did your childhood shape you as a learner and teacher? How has identity, your sense of self, and the culturally imposed narrative of your identity slowed or fueled your journey? If these questions regarding identity do not resonate, simply keep them in mind as you read. We will explore identity and teaching throughout the book.

## Audience

This book is intended for higher education faculty (undergraduate and graduate), as well as student affairs practitioners, academic advisers, and college counselors. Adult educators outside of higher education will also find this book relevant.

## Pronouns

Throughout this book I use a combination of gendered and gender-neutral pronouns to include the full range of gender identities.

## Overview of Chapters

*Connected Teaching* is organized with practitioners in mind. Thus, part one is focused on application, whereas part two dives more deeply into the self-knowledge and reflection essential in connected teaching.

After an introduction to connected teaching, part one, "Connected Teaching in Action," moves to practice topics. Chapter 1, an important foundation for the rest of the book, extends the introduction as a primer on the foundational concepts of RCT and connected teaching. Chapter 2 addresses a pervasive question: How can we teach relationally when there are so many demands on our time? In chapter 3, I consider boundaries in the digital age. Next, chapter 4 offers a relational approach to assessment. In chapter 5, I address disruption and resistance.

Part two, "Increasing Self-Awareness in Connected Teaching," provides a look at the deeper elements of connected teaching. In chapter 6, I focus on power and identity in teaching. Chapter 7 extends this deeper work as we seek to understand transference and move toward relational clarity. In chapter 8, I explore disappointment and failure in teaching. And in chapter 9, I offer an intellectual mattering framework. Finally, in conclusion, I consider teaching as life's work and the journey to honor those who inspired us to learn and eventually teach.

# ACKNOWLEDGMENTS

I have a big team and a deep bench—an amazing group of mentors, colleagues, friends, family, and others who have each played a role in this endeavor.

Judith V. Jordan and Laurent A. Parks Daloz—I am honored by your contributions. Judy—our monthly energizing conversations have deepened my understanding of Relational-Cultural Theory (RCT) and helped me work out some of the more complex challenges that emerged in the writing. Larry, whom I came to know late in this process—your generosity of spirit conveyed through your enthusiasm for this book and your gentle guidance regarding the publishing process has been a tremendous gift.

Sandie Turner, Elizabeth Holloway, Dee Flaherty, Maureen Walker, Lisa Frey, Jennifer Snyder-Duch, and Melanie Booth—you are a dream team of readers, each with a keen critical eye, an encouraging touch, and your own specific areas of expertise. I hope you can see your suggestions, guidance, and knowledge reflected throughout these pages. Beyond your contributions to this book, you are all amazing people and bring significant warmth, insight, and energy to my life. Sandie—special thanks to you for being my trusted first reader of very rough early drafts. You waded through the mud and helped me develop structure and see the possibilities.

Several other people contributed, each in their own unique way. Lisa Graham, Gail Walker, Amy Obusek, Sally Friedman, Indira Nair, the Riley-Hoffmans, the Gruenspechts, the Harrises, and Marcie Gerson—you help me stay grounded, think about the big work, and remain connected with all that is important and good in the world. Gratitude to so many wonderful Jean Baker Miller Training Institute colleagues, particularly Erica Seidel, Shannon Finn, and Audra Sbarra—valued friends and colleagues—you welcomed me into the RCT community and helped me find my place. Kevin Ferra—thanks for an important conversation early in the process. And Elizabeth Holloway, Laurien Alexandre, Denny Golden, Bill Horvath, and Roberta O'Connor—teachers who became mentors and friends—at critical moments you have expanded my sense of who I could become and what I might contribute. Any difference I make is an extension of all you and others have taught me.

Gratitude and hello to my current, former, and future students! You are the center of it all—you are the reason! And to my colleagues at Carlow

University—you give Carlow its heart and soul. Your dedication to education and student well-being is exemplary.

Thanks to the Stylus team. Editor David Brightman—this book would simply not be what it is without your involvement and expertise. Thanks also to managing production editor Alexandra Hartnett, designer Kathleen Dyson, and copy editor Nicole Hirschman.

Finally, much love to my family. Mom and Dad—thanks for always asking, "How's the book coming?" Your support is a never-ending presence in my life. Gratitude from the heart to my grandmothers, each who in her own way believed in me and supported my writing and dreams. Cousin Marilyn—your teaching stories inspire me, and I love talking with you about the work. Thanks to Howard and Joan for keeping an eye on eastern Pennsylvania. Love to Sara and Ed. Shout-out to my kids—Molly and Ryan, Caroline and Chris—and to my grands—Alice and Victoria (who advised me to make it silly and use the word *bluurf*) and Marshall (whom I imagine will agree with his sisters' advice . . . when he learns to talk). Love to Toby the beagle, always sleeping nearby and ready for the next walk. And, finally, to Brenda—I'm grateful every day that I get to live life with you.

# INTRODUCTION

Our roles and lives as professors are scrutinized and changing. Budget cuts mean more work for fewer people. Politicians and popular discourse question the role of higher education. We face pressure for constant evolution in a technology-rich and ever-changing culture. We are expected to be fluent in the classroom and online in a teaching context that may still include chalkboards and requires competence with learning management systems; some of us are expected to transfer courses that we have taught for years in the classroom to the online environment. Whether we are among those who embrace technology or those who dread it, students expect 24/7 accessibility, and the smartphone is often a venue not only for communicating with faculty but also for reading and responding to assignments. There are also students for whom technology is an obstacle because of mind-set or finances, and we need to manage that too.

The digital age has helped shape a new generation of students. Some millennials respond to authority with less deference than previous generations, even viewing the syllabus or an A- as negotiable. Regardless of whether we as faculty are willing to negotiate assignments and grades, the faculty role is changing. Our authority is less top-down and more dynamic, more about artful presence. While some provocateurs would suggest the faculty role is becoming obsolete, I argue that our role as teachers is as important as ever and is evolving profoundly. Our authority is shifting from vertical to horizontal. Understanding our inner lives as teachers and our relational stance and practice with students is vital, as increasingly our role is less about transmitting information and more about inviting learning and shaping the nuance of dynamic learning spaces.

I believe relationships are central to this work—the relationships we have with individual students and with classes and cohorts. I believe relationship is the fulcrum and the spark, the valley and the vista—the essential driver of teaching and learning.

My ongoing quest to understand relationship as a central force in teaching propels this book. I am drawn to those moments of energetic deep learning and all that makes these powerful moments possible—as relationship, identity, and emotion form the heart of connected teaching. We must be open to and seek relationship, understand our sociocultural identity (and how this shapes our internal experience and the ways in which we are met in the world), and vigilantly explore and recognize our emotion in the teaching endeavor. These elements—relationship, identity, and emotion—form the foundation of connected teaching.

In the following section, I situate connected teaching among the writings that have most influenced this work. Next, I introduce Relational-Cultural Theory (RCT), a foundation of this book, and then I explore sociocultural identity and emotion, as they relate to connected teaching.

## Relationship as Essential in Teaching and Learning

Though they are not often acknowledged in the teaching literature, Black women activist educators including Nannie Helen Burroughs, Anna Julia Cooper, and Septima Clark identified relationship as important in teaching and learning. Burroughs, Cooper, and Clark began their careers teaching children and later played significant roles in shaping adult and higher education. In 1901, Burroughs founded the school that would become The National Trade and Professional School for Women and Girls (NTPS), an institution that offered Black girls and women access to junior high, high school, vocational training, and junior college (Johnson, 2000); she served as president until her death in 1961 (Easter-Smith, 2015). Cooper, educated at Oberlin College, Columbia University, and later the Sorbonne, taught at Wilberforce University in Ohio and later served as the second president of Frelinghuysen University in Washington DC, from 1930 to 1941 (Johnson, 2000). Clark created and led programs, including The Citizenship Schools in the 1950s and 1960s, to educate southern African American adults (Charron, 2009).

Burroughs, Cooper, and Clark recognized relationships as essential for teaching and learning. For example, Clark's Citizenship Schools were based on the relationships between educators and their communities. "Every Citizenship School teacher came from the community in which she taught and began class by asking her neighbors what they wanted to learn" (Charron, 2009, p. 6). Burroughs lived her commitment to forming relationships with her students at NTPS where she knew students by name and knew of their families, dined with students, and talked with them about their grades and personal matters (Downey, cited in Johnson, 2000). Each of these women were known as caring educators, committed to their students' success (Charron, 2009; Johnson, 2000).

Though these early educators saw connection as fundamental, a deep consideration of relationship as central in higher learning has been largely absent in the literature. There is no dearth of literature positioning education as a process between teacher and student; however, education scholars have typically focused on understanding the learner, learning theories, and practice (e.g., Cross, 1981; Mezirow & Associates, 1990, 2000; Weimer, 2013). Although these writers often see learning as a process between teacher and student, they tend to focus on understanding the background and learning experience of students rather than on what goes on between teacher and learner. Rarely overlooking the topic completely, some of these essential books include chapters on the teaching relationship, but rarely is this a central focus.

bell hooks, Laurent A. Parks Daloz, Parker Palmer, and Stephen Brookfield changed the conversation, exploring in greater depth what goes on between teachers and students. Building on the work of Paulo Freire and Thich Nhat Hanh, hooks writes from a personal place and considers relational themes including excitement, presence, and care. "To teach in a manner that respects and cares for the souls of our students is essential if we are to provide the necessary conditions where learning can most deeply and intimately begin" (hooks, 1994, p. 13). Where others discuss the importance of engaging students in reflection (thus focusing on students), hooks understands the role of relationship and identifies the import of teacher self-disclosure for engaging student reflection.

> Professors who expect students to share confessional narratives but who are themselves unwilling to share are exercising power in a manner that could be coercive. . . . It is often productive if professors take the first risk, linking confessional narratives to academic discussions so as to show how experience can illuminate and enhance our understanding of academic material. (hooks, 1994, p. 21)

For hooks, education is about transgressing the constraints of race, gender, and class. Thus, her presence in the lives of students must not replicate prevailing power structures. If in her role as a teacher, she reifies a power-over position with her students, she further entrenches the very dynamics she seeks to confront. To teach students to challenge systems of power, privilege, and marginalization, she must interrogate her place in the lives of her students. hooks shows us a way forward, an example of working to undo tacit assumptions about power while also holding on to the roles and responsibilities of teaching. Brookfield also explored power and identity in teaching, from his perspective as a white male, first in 1995 with *Becoming a Critically Reflective Teacher* and then with additional depth and insight in the book's second edition, published in 2017.

Daloz focuses extensively on the relationship between educator and student. He considers teaching as mentoring, "a special kind of relationship, a caring stance in the context of our students' lives" (Daloz, 1999, p. 15). Teacher mentors provide support, challenge, and vision; they help us recognize our moments of transition and transformation; and they welcome us to a new world (Daloz, 1999). Daloz (1999) suggests that significant teacher mentors accompany us on the learning journey and serve as proof that the journey is doable (p. 207). The first time I read Daloz, I understood this to mean that mentors help us transition *to a new sense of self* that develops as we learn or make a career change. More recently, I imagine he might infer something deeper, that teacher mentors help us *into the uncertainty of learning*, through the transitional period of (often) greater confusion and a sense of not knowing. And then they help us to the other side in which we might adjust our sense of self and honor our insatiable desire to continue learning.

Like Daloz and Brookfield, Palmer has inspired generations of teachers. In *The Courage to Teach: Exploring the Inner Landscape of a Teacher's Life* (Palmer, 1998), he also explores the inner lives of teachers and the teaching space as a relational space. Like Daloz, Palmer (1998) pushes us to explore "the inner landscape of the teaching self" (p. 4), including intellectual, emotional, and spiritual paths.

> As important as methods may be, the most practical thing we can achieve in any kind of work is insight into what is happening inside us as we do it. The more familiar we are with our inner terrain, the more surefooted our teaching—and living—becomes. (p. 5)

Palmer (1998) elevates the importance of self-awareness and identity not only for teaching but also for living—reinforcing his call for authenticity and the integrity of wholeness.

Palmer (1998) suggests "good teachers possess a capacity for connectedness" (p. 11), and they connect with students not through their teaching methods but "in their hearts—meaning heart in its ancient sense, as the place where intellect and emotion and spirit will converge in the human self" (p. 11). He illustrates his premise with the image of the heart as a loom on which a fabric is created, a fabric that connects teacher and students, the fabric of a learning community. For Palmer, the teacher's integrity and the fabric of trust, woven *with* students, provide the foundation that make challenge and support possible.

> In the undivided self, every major thread of one's life experience is honored, creating a weave of such coherence and strength that it can hold students and subject as well as self. Such a self, inwardly integrated, is able to make the outward connections on which good teaching depends. (p. 15)

Brookfield (1995), Mezirow and Associates (2000), and Weimer (2013) also consider the relational space in teaching. Brookfield (1995), pushing us to be critically reflective teachers, warns against "teaching innocently" (p. 1) or without interrogating our intentions, actions, and assumptions about the effect we have on our students. He recognizes vulnerability, imperfection, power, and identity as inevitable elements of the teaching experience (Brookfield, 2015, 2017). Like Daloz and Palmer, Mezirow and Associates (2000) speak of teacher identity and the importance of supportive relationships in teaching and learning. Similarly, Weimer (2010) describes the internal elements of good teaching: "emotional energy, the will to keep caring, intellectual stamina, creative approaches, vigilance, faith in the power of feedback to prompt learning, and perseverance to find the way back from failure" (p. xi).

While hooks inextricably links identity and teaching, Daloz's awareness of the influence that race, gender, class, and other forms of identity play in teaching relationships increased over time. In the 2012 update to his seminal *Mentor: Guiding the Journey of Adult Learners*, Daloz acknowledges that he seeks to remove "some of my more sexist assumptions" (p. xxiv).

I aspire to follow hooks's lead to remain vigilant regarding the influence of identity in the teaching relationship. RCT, the human development theory at the heart of this book, calls on us to hold social constructions of identity and cultural context as central to understanding relational practice.

## A Brief Introduction to RCT

RCT fits naturally as a framework to help us understand meaningful academic interactions and relationships. Indeed, the founding scholars proclaimed that growth-in-relation happens not only in therapy but also at work and school and in friendships (Miller & Stiver, 1997). They describe the rich mutuality of meaningful exchanges between people in particular roles (therapist and client, teacher and student) and among colleagues, friends, and family members who are present with each other, listen closely, and respond with respect.

> Because each person can receive and then respond to the feelings and thoughts of the other, each is able to enlarge both her own feelings and thoughts *and* the feelings and thoughts of the other person. Simultaneously, each person enlarges the relationship. (Miller & Stiver, 1997, p. 29)

At first glance, Miller and Stiver's words may seem to be a routine description of typical conversation, of people listening and responding to each other. However, I believe that their insight is in recognizing that meaningful interactions extend each person's sense of self and experience (and the relationship).

That is to say, the key to growth-in-relation is that we expand each other's world. In the context of teaching, an interaction may seem either mundane (clarifying an assignment) or potentially life changing (encouraging a student to consider doctoral study). Big or small, these moments potentially broaden a student's landscape of understanding and possibility. Though not an RCT scholar, Mayeroff (1971) suggests that in patient caring, we give "the other room to live" and we expand "the other's living room" (p. 24). Perhaps in teaching, we expand each other's learning space.

Jean Baker Miller launched the development of what would become RCT in 1976 with her publication *Toward a New Psychology of Women* in which she argued that Western culture's privileging of the individual self over relationships was built on a male model of development and was damaging to the well-being of both women and men. She argued that by celebrating and prioritizing the self rather than relationships, our culture encourages people to separate rather than connect and to believe in the myth of solo achievement. The value of connection and relationships is at the heart of this book.

Miller, a psychiatrist, began collaborating with three psychologists, Irene Stiver, Judith Jordan, and Janet Surrey, developing what was initially called Stone Center Theory, later named self-in-relation theory, and then relational theory (Jordan, 2010). In 1981, they began presenting and publishing, as they introduced Stone Center Theory to relevant academic and professional communities. They were met with resistance but continued, and over time additional scholar-practitioners, including Maureen Walker and Amy Banks, joined the growing movement. Readers may see parallels between RCT and Carol Gilligan's work. RCT scholars and Gilligan and her students, all located in eastern Massachusetts, connected and shared their work at biannual "Learning From Women" conferences, sponsored by Harvard Medical School (Jordan, 2010). Later in the 1980s, Belenky, Clinchy, Goldberger, and Tarule published the first edition of *Women's Ways of Knowing: The Development of Self, Voice, and Mind*. Belenky and her colleagues briefly mention a connected teaching model, an approach similar to contemporary notions of learner-centered teaching in which the expert seeks to understand the learner and establish trust.

From the start, Miller saw the role of gender in power dynamics, exposing and challenging the power that men held collectively and individually over women in a male-dominated and male-centric culture (Jordan, 2010). As new thinkers joined the movement, they pushed Miller and the other founding scholars to think beyond gender.

Early RCT theory was skewed by the fact that the original writers were all white, middle class, and well educated. While these writers as women protested the distortions imposed mostly by men on a psychology of women, they unfortunately duplicated this distortion by talking about women's voice rather than women's voices, revealing how the assumption of universality by the privileged dominant group creeps in to even the most conscious attempts to incorporate diversity and appreciate power inequities. Women of color, lesbians, other sexually identified women, physically challenged women, and women from different economic backgrounds personally communicated . . . that "the theory group" was committing the very distortions of exclusion they were protesting. (Jordan, 2010, p. 11)

This early resistance within the relational theory community led to another name change in the theory's evolution, and relational theory became RCT, an acknowledgment and ongoing reminder that in relationship, people bring their experience of cultural context and that the relationship itself always occurs within the larger cultural context.

## Identity—I'm More Aware of Being White Than I Used to Be

What does being white have to do with teaching and teaching relationships? Typically, we are far less aware of our identities that grant privilege than those that bring marginalization, discrimination, hate, and violence. I do not have to think about being white to avoid race-related confrontation in my daily life, whereas colleagues and students of color often do. Conversely, I *am* aware of being a Jew and gay. I am routinely aware of being a woman and less cognizant of being cisgender. Previously, I worked in institutions that were largely class privileged and was far more aware of my middle/working-class roots than I am now, teaching at Carlow University, more of a first-generation space.

Identity invokes privilege and marginalization and thus shapes learning environments and teaching relationships. When I understand both the power and the marginalization imposed by my identities, I become a better educator, as I am more likely to recognize: obstacles and injustices faced regularly by students, the manifestations of power and marginalization in my relationships with students, and the limits that my worldview potentially levies on my teaching and thus my teaching relationships (Brookfield, 2017; hooks, 1994). This last element may be the most difficult to grasp; it relates to Brookfield's caution about "teaching innocently" or without an awareness that our teaching and advising may not be received by students as we intend.

## Teaching and Emotion

To authentically and effectively be in relation with our students, we must also strive to know ourselves well. In addition to understanding the influence of our own social identity locations, we are more effective when we know ourselves emotionally and understand our tendencies and patterns when working with students. Douglas Robertson, a leading scholar of college teaching and emotion, proposed that only an intersubjective approach can accurately unpack the teaching–learning dynamic, and to understand the process of good teaching, we must consider what is going on not only for our learners but also for ourselves as teachers (Robertson, 1996, 1997, 1999a, 1999b, 2001a). Stated more simply, the question is not whether teaching is an emotional experience but whether we acknowledge or deny the emotion inherent in teaching (Robertson, 1996, 1997, 1999a, 1999b, 2001a; Schwartz & Holloway, 2017; Slater, Veach, & Li, 2013; Snyder-Duch, 2018).

Emotions are central in the teaching experience. Consider the following two examples:

1. I am reading a student's dissertation draft and realize that I am disproportionally agitated by errors and absence of American Psychological Association (APA) style. I continue reading, and my frustration grows. Finally, I realize I am too annoyed to read clearly for content, and I put the draft aside. Later, I identify my frustration and its source—I feel as if the student is wasting my time; it is late in the semester, I am tired, I have a lot of work and want to get this done; the APA problems slow my process. I remind myself that the student is in the early stages of her work, and I can refer her to the learning center for help with APA style. Later, I return to the draft and read for content. Finally, upon further reflection, I challenge my perception that the student was wasting my time, a frame that inaccurately personalizes the process of reviewing student work—she was not doing anything to me—and the view that she was wasting my time likely increased my agitation.

2. The class is Social and Cultural Context of Counseling. I ask students to write a reflection in response to our discussion on race, a discussion immediately following several police killings of unarmed Black men and in the heat of the 2016 presidential election. I see one white student sitting with her arms folded, refusing to engage (at least in writing). In my mind, I acknowledge my concern that she will walk out of the room. I also know I am invested in wanting students (particularly white students) to at least consider the role that race plays in their experience, and I

know I sometimes feel frustrated when they resist. By quickly naming my emotions and not judging them, I am able to remain steady despite the tension in the room. I recall several of this student's previous comments and realize that if she is at all willing to engage with these ideas, she might need to do so outside the classroom; she may not even be ready to engage in the internal process of writing as she sits with her peers and me. I give her space. She does not leave the room and sits quietly through the follow-up discussion. I do not know to what degree she considered the perspectives shared subsequently by her classmates; however, I know I was able to reframe my assumptions about what she was thinking and to maintain my focus in the classroom.

Throughout this book, I share moments like the first where I had to step away and reflect to sort myself out, and other experiences like the second where I responded effectively in the moment. I also share thoughts about the kinds of student interactions that continue to challenge me and about experiences of failure. The point is, I am a more effective teacher when I can identify my emotional responses to subpar work and excellent work and to student disengagement, over-engagement, push-back, complaint, joy, and unexpected interest in me and my work. Self-awareness makes me a better teacher. And striving for greater self-awareness is an ongoing journey. The quest toward greater understanding of emotion and teaching is another thread throughout this book.

## Onward

Our profession provides an opportunity to engage in dynamic relationships wherein we come to know ourselves more clearly, refine our approaches to teaching, deepen our thinking, and find a place of mattering in the world. Our role and priority as teachers is first and foremost to focus on student learning. However, if we are open to being changed and influenced, the journeys we take with our students can be life changing for us as well.

# PART ONE

## CONNECTED TEACHING
## IN ACTION

# I

# WHAT IS CONNECTED
# TEACHING?

What does it mean to connect with students? What does connection look like given that much of the work of teaching and learning is solitary? At the same time, how do we think about connection in the digital age when some students seem to expect us to be available almost 24/7?

In this chapter, I explore the significance of relationship in teaching and learning. Next, I illuminate three central Relational-Cultural Theory (RCT) concepts that serve as building blocks for the rest of this book and, more broadly, connected teaching: relationship as a site and source for learning, power-over and power-with, and relational clarity.

As described in the introduction, Jean Baker Miller and the founding RCT scholars challenged the prevailing Western idea that autonomy is the goal of adult development. Instead they proposed we are at our best when we have the capacity to engage in and maintain growth-fostering relationships (Miller & Stiver, 1997). Relational capacity and competence are the goals of development, and through connection with others we become our most authentic, creative, and productive selves (Jordan, 2010; Miller & Stiver, 1997; Surrey, 1985; Walker, 2004).

The RCT focus on relationship as central is not intended to disregard the reality that learning and teaching require self-direction, discipline, and solitary work. Rather, I believe the founders were pushing us to challenge the cultural glorification of self-reliance by admitting that the narratives of lone heroes and individual achievers are inaccurate, failing to acknowledge the colleagues, spouses, friends, benefactors, and others who contribute to success. RCT does not negate the hard work and solitary hours inherent in the lives of teachers and students. However, this individual effort is not the whole story.

As I write this book (a far too solitary endeavor!), I spend hours alone thinking, struggling, writing, and rewriting. RCT would not discount this solo work. RCT would, however, have me acknowledge that I am able to write this book in part because my wife gives me space to do the work and she encourages me when I doubt myself or feel frustrated or tired. Likewise, when I feel stuck in my thinking, I turn to close trusted colleagues—they do not solve the intellectual puzzles for me but join me in my wandering and wondering. My former department head, now retired, reads very rough first drafts and provides feedback. Several of my friends and colleagues read specific chapters and provide invaluable critique and encouragement. I do not do this alone.

The RCT focus on relationship allows me to avoid getting stuck in the idea that I *should* do this alone. I share the stories of those who help me, attempting to demystify the appearance of lone achievement that can cause others, students, for example, to feel as if they fail if they cannot achieve alone. A lifetime of building relationships gives me a solid set of resources critical to writing this book—I am convinced that if I did not have these people around me, this book would have been more of a struggle and less developed (or might not have come to fruition).

At the same time, we are not always literally in relationship (Surrey, 1985). RCT suggests relationship rather than separation as an organizing principle and concurrently acknowledges that we are not always in active connection with others. Applying RCT in the educational realm, I propose that relationship implies the *availability* of intellectual and emotional connection. We are not always connected to our students, nor they to us. But ideally they experience us as relationally available to them, accessible for connection. This does not indicate we are literally and infinitely available for a text or call. Nor does it imply that teaching and learning relationships do not occasionally include misunderstandings and conflict. However, in connected teaching, our students ultimately trust that we will reply to them with regard and a commitment to their learning.

This is a deeper sense of availability than "if I e-mail her, she will respond." Rather, it is the sense that if a student contacts me, I will be intellectually and emotionally available and receptive. I will neither dismiss nor shame the student who does not understand something. I will not judge the student who is afraid of failure. I will meet the student's curiosity and dreams with enthusiasm. I will offer valid and valuable critique. When I realize that I was not as effective in class or as present on a video call as I intended to be, I will reflect and attempt to do better next time. I will meet students with respect, commitment to their learning, openness, and enthusiasm. I will constantly strive to become a better teacher. I will share the reality of the scholarly life (joy and frustration, collaboration and solitude, obstacles and insight). And I will provide students with challenge and support as I strive to help them strive. In it all, I will honor their humanity and my own.

A relational teacher is attentive and responsive with students; this intent and ability to connect is inherent in all aspects of teaching—creating an online learning space, setting the tone in the classroom, and structuring and assessing assignments. Relational teaching is not simply a strategy we enact when we are advising; rather it is the foundation of the entire teaching endeavor. Relational practice is evident in single meaningful interactions and longer term teaching relationships (Cress, 2008; Giles, 2011; Hoffman, 2014; Karpouza & Emvalotis, 2018; Liang, Tracy, Kauh, Taylor, & Williams, 2006; Liang, Tracy, Taylor, & Williams, 2002; McMillan-Roberts, 2014; Schwartz, 2009; Schwartz & Holloway, 2014, 2017).

Connected teaching is also evident in "the teacher in my head." When I am working alone as a writer, I sometimes think something through with one of my teachers or colleagues simply present in my internal conversation. This can happen when I imagine this person as available to me, that they would be receptive if I reached out. But if I were to worry this person would dismiss or ridicule me, then I would experience the kind of unhealthy separation and isolation described by RCT (Jordan, 1990, 2010).

> It is not through separation, but through more highly articulated and expanded relational experience that individual development takes place. . . . By relationship I mean an experience of emotional and cognitive intersubjectivity: the ongoing intrinsic inner awareness and responsiveness to the continuous existence of the other or others, and the expectation of mutuality in this regard. (Surrey, 1985, p. 6)

Intellectual and emotional availability between teachers and students is central in productive teaching, learning, and other intellectual endeavors. In RCT parlance, when we experience growth-fostering interactions, we build a base of psychological resources that help us through subsequent moments of conflict and disconnection (Miller, 1986). Applied to teaching and learning, growth-fostering interactions and the experience of teachers and colleagues as intellectually and emotionally available may be one of the most important and yet least recognized resources for the intellectual and emotional journey taken by students and teachers alike. The foundation that I develop through meaningful interactions with trusted mentors, teachers, and colleagues is part of the internal strength that drives me when I am working alone, feeling frustrated, considering intellectual risks, playing with ideas, and aspiring to reach beyond what I once imagined I could do.

## Three Fundamental Ideas

In the following sections, I explore three foundational elements of RCT as they relate to teaching. First, I examine relationship as a site and source for learning. Second, I analyze power in the teaching and learning relationship through an RCT lens. Third, I consider relational clarity.

### *Relationship as a Site and Source for Learning*

Connected teaching consists of and creates five elements that drive learning: energy, knowledge, sense of worth, action, and desire for more connection. Readers familiar with RCT will recognize these as The Five Good Things, as first identified by Miller and Stiver (1997). These components are both essence and outcome as they form the heart of what goes on in connected teaching and are further generated by meaningful interactions and relationships.

*Energy.* How does connection increase energy? Most obvious perhaps is the additive nature of vigorous intellectual dialogue. However, beyond simply building on each other's ideas, two people who are deeply engaged with each other experience a joining with, a connection that validates each person's relevance and legitimacy as teacher and student (Edwards & Richards, 2002; McMillian-Roberts, 2014; Schwartz, 2013, 2017; Schwartz & Holloway, 2012, 2014, 2017). As I bring my best intellectual self to a student and respond with enthusiasm, I convey to the student, "You, in this moment, the person you are with these thoughts and emotionality, I see your worth, and I want to share this learning moment with you." My energy in turn activates the student's energy as she can more fully be herself and take intellectual risks. And sometimes students light the spark and their energy invigorates us. This is mutuality in teaching and learning.

Positive psychology (Fredrickson, 2001) suggests that positive emotions such as joy and curiosity position us to think creatively, while emotions such as fear and anger initiate a fight-or-flight response and narrow our thinking to focus on survival. Positive emotions poise us to be open, take risks, and think broadly—and to be creative. Healthy and meaningful academic connections enhance these positive states, and then relationship and positive emotions combine to facilitate students' creativity, intellectual growth, and increased confidence.

*Knowledge.* Just as passionate intellectual dialogue clearly generates new knowledge or knowing, so can routine teaching interactions. Those brief e-mail exchanges or conversations after class that help students understand assignments or apply learning may not in and of themselves shift a paradigm or change a life, but often they keep the batteries charged and combine for bigger knowing. These short, focused interactions enhance a student's repertoire and knowledge (of both self and discipline). Students experience these interactions as powerful because they are moments of reconstruction rather than simply rote or additive learning. "At times this moment is about reconstructing knowledge, coming to understand a concept at a deeper level or with more complexity. Elsewhere, this moment is about reconstructing self, coming to understand one's self differently" (Schwartz & Holloway, 2012, p. 127). Sometimes the fire is started by a lightning bolt and other times by a series of small sparks. Reconstructing is learning in its most dynamic form and is the experience that animates students (Schwartz & Holloway, 2012).

*Sense of worth.* Students experience an increased sense of worth when teachers respond to them in a manner that seems beyond just doing one's job. We feel validated and aware of our own worth when someone welcomes us, joins with us, and responds to our unique being, thoughts, and feelings (Giles, 2011; Karpouza & Emvalotis, 2018; Schwartz, 2013; Schwartz & Holloway, 2012, 2014). In part, this manifests as intellectual mattering, though intellectual mattering is not the only dynamic that increases students' sense of worth.

In addition, students see themselves more positively when they realize they are not alone in their struggles and when they feel challenged by a professor. Faculty who self-disclose stories of their own experiences as students, wrestling with content or the difficulty of balancing work, school, and family, help students contextualize their own trials. Students realize they are not failing or incapable but rather encountering obstacles inherent in the learning experience (Schwartz & Holloway, 2012). In addition, students who feel respectfully challenged by engaged faculty are more likely to be open to assessment and feedback and to experience critique as a sign of their worth and potential rather than failure and shame (Schwartz, 2009, 2017).

Finally, these interactions and relationships increase educators' sense of worth as well (Karpouza & Emvalotis, 2018; McMillian-Roberts, 2014; Schwartz, 2013; Schwartz & Holloway, 2012, 2017). In that moment when students have found me helpful, I know that my presence in the exchange was valuable, and so in helping, I am validated (I should not need or invite students to validate me, but acknowledging that I experience affirmation through good teaching exchanges helps me maintain relational clarity). When a student seems energized and more focused after we talk, I sense that I am right where I need to be. "People tend to feel empowered and worthy if they feel they have an effect—an impact—on others" (Miller & Stiver, 1997, p. 35).

*Action or movement.* Creative thinking, growth, and a boost in confidence spark the student toward action. This is most obvious in positive and enthusiastic interactions, such as when a student meets to clarify a paper topic and leaves with ideas, energy, and a plan—he is positioned to move forward on the paper. The link between connection and movement is also evident though perhaps less obvious when students are mired in the difficulty of their work or academic journey. Think of a time when you met with a student who was slightly upset or frustrated, perhaps not understanding course content or feeling overwhelmed and unsure about continuing in the program. You meet with the student and discuss the challenge. Often, students seem lighter and more optimistic at the end of these meetings; this response is so typical it hardly seems noteworthy, and yet rarely is the problem fully resolved or the work completed.

So why does the student feel a little better? Because connection and all that it brings help people get unstuck. This is significant for all students, particularly for adults trying to move through their academic programs amidst the challenges of balancing family, work, and school (Kasworm, 2008). Through engaged conversation and real presence, we convey to students that they matter and their challenges are real and can be overcome. Connection boosts energy and is a forum to begin to solve problems, and this moves the student from feeling stuck or paralyzed to seeing a step forward. The power of connection to fuel movement may be one of the most important yet overlooked aspects of teaching. As we will see in chapter 2, we do not need time-intensive long-term relationships to engage in these kinds of powerful relational moments; these can happen in one-off interactions as well.

*Desire for more connection.* Experiencing our multifaceted selves in mutual regard with another person pushes away our doubts and reinforces that our deep struggles and big ideas (and the less noteworthy moments in between) are valid. Connection helps us get unstuck, move forward, and see our own value; these positive experiences prompt us to seek more connection with each other and with others in our academic and professional worlds. RCT proposes "the goal is not for the individual to grow out of relationships, but to grow into them" (Miller & Stiver, 1997, p. 22).

## Power-Over and Power-With

Writing primarily about the ways in which a male-normed and male-privileging society subordinates women, Jean Baker Miller interrogated the hegemony of the male-dominant culture. Her insight helped women understand how, for example, the surrounding culture led them to devalue their roles as caregivers and to discount the meaning and life-sustaining energy they found in relationships. Miller sought to redefine *power*:

For women today, power may be defined as "the capacity to implement."
. . . This has not been the meaning of "power" in the past. Power has generally meant the ability to advance oneself and, simultaneously, to control,
limit, and if possible, destroy the power of others. That is, power, so far,
has had at least two components: power *for* oneself and power *over* others.
(There is an important distinction between the ability to influence others
and the power to control and restrict them.) (Miller, 1986, p. 116)

Miller (1986) continued, "Women start, however, from a position in which
they have been dominated" (p. 117). This reality lingers. Even for children
raised in homes where parents model egalitarian adult partnerships (perhaps
more important in opposite-sex couples in terms of conveying equality),
children encounter gender stereotypes and power dynamics in school. And
even if they escape this in the classroom and on the playground, children
are surrounded by a culture that still shows men as mighty and women as
seen through the male gaze, a culture wherein when they are old enough to
understand, they will realize that on average an equally qualified woman will
earn less for doing the same job as a man.

    While Miller framed the argument around gender, other founding RCT
scholars extended her work, arguing that people of color; people with dis-
abilities; lesbian, gay, bisexual, transgender, and queer (LGBTQ) people; and
those living in poverty are also marginalized and experience emotional and
physical violence enacted by people and systems (consciously or not) seeking to perpetuate their power. And as I write this, I am reminded daily that
immigrants, refugees, Muslims, and Jews also face these levels of discrimination; marginalization; disadvantage; and sometimes hate, violence, and mur-
der. In the multiple intersectional ways that many of us have identities that
are not dominant or privileged, we start from a place of being marginalized.

    Before I continue to unpack how RCT helps us understand the inter-
play between power, cultural context, and teaching and learning, I want to
pause and focus on power in the teaching and learning relationship. All other
things being equal (meaning all aspects of identity), a teacher clearly holds
power over students—position power, power inherent in the assessment role,
and often power regarding a student's future (e.g., letters of recommendation, networking, and even adviser problem-solving). When teaching power
is used to dominate or control (even unintentionally), we diminish the learning space. A student who feels controlled or limited by fear will likely be less
creative, take fewer risks, and perhaps choose a safer academic path.

    Turning again to the interplay between power, cultural context, and
teaching and learning, in terms of identity all things are not typically equal.
A white male student feels entitled to challenge the authority of a professor

who is a woman of color. Or a transgender student is afraid to ask for help because his professor previously declined to use his preferred name and pronouns. Attending to the power differentials created by identity is not just about diversity and inclusion as expressions of personal, organizational, and institutional values but also about understanding that identity means some people start from a place of subordination that may very well tell them that they do not belong and do not have a right to the empowering relationships available to the dominant class. Ironically, our culture conveys that relationships are a women's thing and not important for men. However, the career-boosting, wealth-building, and often politically valuable connections made by men in elite schools, over drinks, and on the golf course prove otherwise. Our culture pretends that some people, particularly heterosexual white men, make it on their own, but indeed they benefit greatly from and sometimes revel in their social, career, and political networks. Culture reinforces the myth of the self-made man, but as noted early in this chapter, the reality is that any successful person has been helped, taught, encouraged, and possibly financially supported by others.

Returning to Miller (1986), we learn that beginning from a place of marginalization requires people to find at least a small base of power from which to start to move out of subordination and disadvantage. Finding that power (often in connection) can be seen as a threat to members of the dominant class (and even to others in the marginalized group who fear they will get left behind). So, taking the step forward, away from marginalization and toward empowerment requires risking further isolation and loss of connection. What does this have to do with teaching? Miller's understanding of power (and additional insight brought forth by the colleagues who pushed her and the other founding scholars to see beyond their race and class privilege) helps us begin to explore often-unseen dynamics in teaching relationships.

### Relational Clarity

Whether we are motivated by a wish to reduce hierarchy in the teaching relationship or the undeniable fact that teachers are no longer the gatekeepers to learning, relational clarity provides structure as we move forward in our work with students. Deeper and more complex than boundaries, relational clarity guides, drives, and indicates growth. In conventional usage, boundaries are about protection and thus reinforce a separation mind-set.

> It isn't that boundaries are bad, but we use the term "boundary" as a code word that obscures the inherent complexity. We all need to think about safety in relationships, the role of power and how that can be used for or against safety. We all have to be clear about what is our experience and the

other person's experience. But when people don't take time to really think about "boundaries," it is used simply and flippantly and it drives people into a separation model. (Jordan, May 24, 2017)

Conversely, we experience relational clarity as we move into the interaction or relationship with a conscious and ever-evolving sense of where our experience and emotion stops and where the student's starts.

For example, one faculty member (unpublished data from Schwartz & Holloway, 2017) recalled experiences early in his career when he took it personally when students declined to work hard in his classes. He remembered feeling frustrated: "I mean, why would you do this to me? I am giving you so much of myself, don't you see what I am trying to do for you?" However, he also noted that as he gained more experience, he realized that students have various degrees of commitment to learning, he does not always know what students might be dealing with that distracts them from school, and ultimately he needs to avoid taking on the disappointment he feels when students do not engage. His early-career perspective represents an absence of relational clarity; he internalized students' experiences of not maximizing their education. However later in his career, he developed the ability to discern between his own experience and student effort.

Another professor in the same study recalled a student who tended to get upset in response to constructive criticism. The professor would allow the student to express her upset (typically by crying) and would then return to the point she was trying to make. In this way, the professor allows room for the student's emotions but does not take them on, become defensive, or recoil from providing feedback. Nor does she move into the role of a therapist; rather she sits with the student, accepting the student's upset but not taking it on as her own. The professor is capable of being with the student and her emotions without shaming or distancing, and she concurrently remains clear on her role as a teacher.

How do we stay with students and their emotion and hold on to our teaching role? Put simply, we must be present enough to hear the student's story and notice the student's affect, remain open to being touched by the student's experience and emotion, and remain clear that the experience is not ours and that our role is that of a teacher. To be truly open to hearing the student and allowing her emotions to touch mine, I must be clear about who I am and who the student is. "This involves temporary identification with the other's state, during which one is aware that the source of the affect is in the other" (Jordan, 1991, p. 69).

The following composite story allows us to explore this balance. I am meeting with an advisee who was not hired as a graduate assistant (GA). She thought she was an ideal candidate and so did I. She was excited that the GA position would allow her to leave her retail job and gain more substantial experience. In addition, I am frustrated with the colleague who did not hire this student, feeling as if he did not see the student's potential. The student is upset. If I distance myself from the student, I will not be able to validate her disappointment. If she feels that I do not understand why she is upset or that I am uncomfortable with students sharing emotions, then she might leave the meeting quickly, and the possibility of this being a learning or transformational moment is gone. While remaining highly separate from her is problematic, so is getting triggered by or absorbing her experience as my own. If her upset sets off my feelings of anger about a time I was not hired, she might feel as if I am unable to really hear her experience without making the moment about me, or she might feel compelled to console me in my upset. In addition, if I take on too much of her upset and begin to feel disappointed on her behalf as well as my own disappointment, I probably will not have the intellectual clarity I need to be a good teacher in this moment.

Instead, I allow her disappointment to touch me. I tell her I remember similar feelings when I have been turned down for jobs. She shares that she is considering quitting the graduate program, fearing she will not reach her goal of a professional career. I disclose that I had similar feelings when I was pursuing a career change that did not transpire. I acknowledge that I processed the experience and disappointment with a trusted mentor and a few friends to help me move on from the setback. I ask the student about the interview, and she admits that it was not her best. As she describes a few of the questions and her responses, I realize that she did not interview well. I encourage her to make an appointment with a career counselor on campus for help with interview preparation.

By remaining open to connection and to her emotion and experience, I opened the door for her to continue sharing and through this I modeled resilience in the face of disappointment and suggested steps for professional development. In growth-fostering interactions we must strive for a balance of connection and relational clarity (Jordan, 1991, 1997). If we remain rigidly separated and closed off, we are unable to understand the student's inner state. Conversely, if we cannot distinguish between the student's emotion and our own, we are equally unable to understand the student's experience. We then get lost in an emotional haze and are unable to operate as teachers. We cannot effectively teach from either of these polarities (Jordan, 1991, 1997; Tom, 1997). Of note, this balance does not come easily.

When we as faculty establish and teach from a place of relational clarity, navigating the magnetisms of connection and separation, we cocreate a space for significant learning and growth.

We are referring to a process which encompasses increasing levels of complexity, choice, fluidity, and articulation within the context of human relationship. What this new model emphasizes is that the direction of growth is not toward greater degrees of autonomy or individuation . . . but toward a process of growth within relationship, where both or all people involved are encouraged and challenged to maintain connection and to foster, adapt, and change with the growth of the other. (Surrey, 1985, p. 5)

As we will explore in later chapters, a relational approach facilitates learning, receptivity to feedback, and intellectual risk-taking. On a deeper level, a relational approach fueled by clarity also promotes development. The navigation of the relationship is itself a growth space, facilitating increased sense of self-in-relation (Jordan, 1991), psychological resources (Miller, 1986), and relational competence (Surrey, 1985). "In a mutually empathic relationship, each individual allows and assists the other to come with focused energy more fully into his or her own truth or reality and into relationship" (Jordan, 1997, p. 53). As we work with students from a place of relational clarity and as we continue to traverse the relational terrain, we promote students' development and refinement of scholar-practitioner identity and relational acumen, while at the same time enhancing our own (Jordan, 1991, 1997; Schwartz, 2011). In the next chapter, I challenge one of the concerns I sometimes hear about the idea of connected teaching—that a relational approach sounds time-intensive. I propose teaching as a relational practice can happen in singular, even brief interactions, as well as in longer term relationships.

# 2

## ONE GOOD EXCHANGE

### Connected Teaching When There Isn't Enough Time

The ubiquity of digital technology in all its forms has created profound shifts in our culture, including perceptions and expectations regarding time. The flexibility afforded by technology suggests we might have more opportunity for greater connection with students, but instead most of us feel as if there is less time than ever for meaningful interactions and deep thinking (Berg & Seeber, 2017; Hogan, 2017). We wonder what students want from connections with faculty; some students seem more interested in a text than a conversation, whereas others convey an intensity of need that can be overwhelming.

In this chapter, I seek to discover the essence of meaningful teaching interactions. First, I look closely at the potential of a single interaction. Second, I explore students' perceptions of time with faculty. Third, I propose invitation, presence, care, and enthusiasm as essential elements in connected teaching.

Our relational presence in the learning space holds tremendous potential as a catalyst for student engagement and learning, even in brief interactions (Fletcher & Ragins, 2007; Giles, 2011; Karpouza & Emvalotis, 2018; Schwartz & Holloway, 2014). For those of us whose formative years were precomputer (or pre-pervasive computing), meaningful connections with faculty likely consisted of lengthy meetings in faculty offices or a local coffee shop and sometimes ongoing or long-term relationships. When these scenarios are no longer likely or possible because of the time crunches faced by students and faculty alike and low-residency, hybrid, and online structures, we are left wondering how we can engage in relational practice. Research suggests meaningful *interactions* are relevant and powerful in students' lives, that we do not have to spend hours and hours with students to make a difference (Fletcher & Ragins, 2007; Giles, 2011; Karpouza & Emvalotis, 2018;

Schwartz & Holloway, 2014). Meaningful interactions help students gain not only clarity regarding course content and assignments but also help develop confidence, metacognition regarding the learning process, and scholar-practitioner identity (Schwartz, 2013; Schwartz & Holloway, 2012, 2014).

In chapter 1, I described the potential of a single meeting to reenergize students and help them move forward. Many of us remember similar experiences, such as a meeting with a graduate adviser or dissertation chair that helped us get unstuck from a moment wherein we felt as if we could not decide a next step or sort out a problem with the research. How do these conversations stimulate progress? Sure, understanding content facilitates movement; however, I propose that presence, care, and enthusiasm are also vital ingredients that help students advance in their studies.

So, if we have not given someone the literal answer to their question, how is it that presence, care, and enthusiasm facilitate movement? Relational-cultural theory (RCT) scholars throughout the history of the theory have claimed that relationships promote growth. But how? Meaningful interactions (singular or as part of a larger relationship) offer a step forward where none existed before.

The following composite narrative provides an example. A student contacts me to say she is coding a transcript and is confused, so we schedule a video call. A few days later, we both sign on and begin the call with a pleasant check-in. Already we both get the subtle message that someone else cares, someone else wishes to engage. This is positive energy.

Next the student begins to explain where she is stuck. Searching for the words to describe her confusion, she gains a little clarity at least about her confusion. This gives her energy and confidence as she begins to understand her situation. I respond by reflecting on the learning curve I experienced as a student, when I started coding. She feels validated and less alone knowing that her struggle is not atypical. I already feel as if I have been helpful, and this gives me a slight boost.

She continues thinking aloud about coding, and I ask questions and clarify. The content of our exchanges seems to help her understand the method and move forward in her work. However, RCT would suggest that there is something deeper occurring. When she initiates our conversation, she moves slightly from her stuck place. When I receive her inquiry with openness, acceptance, and enthusiasm for her work, I am also moving, and as she experiences my open energy, she is encouraged to continue in this intellectual engagement. When we begin the video call and she notices that I am glad to see her and eager to discuss her question, she feels freer to not-know and engage.

> The expectation that someone will listen and make an effort to understand greatly enhances the clarity and sureness of the message presented. . . . If the other is not empathically attuned, disappointment and a sense of being unheard or invalidated results one's sense of clarity diminishes. (Jordan, 1997, pp. 51–52)

If I had appeared frustrated that she did not understand, she may have felt less safe, and this may have stalled the conversation. Instead, she sees me as receptive and begins to describe her confusion. When I share my own story and then we continue discussing the method, a resonance develops, and this affirms and energizes both of us.

If the conversation had gone differently, for example, if I had been distracted, frustrated, or demeaning, she might have left discouraged and unsure about her ability to code and eventually complete her dissertation. Instead, she leaves feeling energized and capable with the knowledge she needs to move forward. In fact, the dialogue itself was movement, and so she is progressing. I leave the conversation affirmed as a teacher and with a new glimpse into an aspect of the method that students may find confusing. I make a mental note to address this preemptively next time I teach coding. So I am moving forward in my teaching. All of this is to say that the power of the interaction was not only instrumental but also about connection and resonance. Connection in and of itself played a role in this meaningful teaching–learning interaction.

However, I want to be clear: There are all kinds of reasons beyond the professor's control why this might have gone differently. Students who are struggling do not always ask for help. The scenario might have been different had I explained the very thing she was asking about several times in online seminars and felt frustrated that she did not understand. Or, she may have been late, unprepared, or directing her frustration at me. All this is to say that I am not claiming that all interactions are meaningful or if we simply approach them in a particular manner, they will lead to connection and movement. Rather I am attempting to illuminate the potential power of single interactions and to illustrate that these engagements have great promise and often carry more import for students than we may understand.

## High-Quality Connections

Jane Dutton affirms the potential of single interactions as she explores high-quality connections in the workplace. She suggests that high-quality connections, or "ties between people marked by mutual regard, trust, and active engagement" (Dutton, 2003, p. xv), increase individual and organizational effectiveness and productivity. Similar to meaningful teaching interactions, Dutton's high-quality connections do not require lengthy meetings or long-term relationships.

> Any point of interaction with another person can potentially be a high-quality connection. One conversation, one e-mail exchange, one moment of connecting in a meeting can infuse both participants with a greater sense of vitality, giving them a bounce in their steps and a greater capacity to act. (Dutton, 2003, p. 2)

Dutton draws on positive psychology and other research on emotions, suggesting that high-quality connections improve physical and psychological health, increase learning, and "give people access to both emotional resources (such as excitement or support) and instrumental resources (such as information) that allow them to engage in their tasks more effectively" (Dutton, 2003, p. 12). In short, high-quality connections fuel our ability to work.

As noted, a commitment to seeking high-quality connections does not imply that we need to spend more time with students. Routine teaching exchanges are potentially high quality (Giles, 2011). For example, students may perceive individualized feedback as an indication of extra time or attention. Individualized feedback conveys commitment to student learning:

> *It was meaningful because I felt that she had really taken time to read my—my project, analyze it, and gave a lot of thought to what could be done to make this project even better. . . . She gave me some very specific suggestions. —Maggie* (Schwartz & Holloway, 2014, p. 45)

While most teaching faculty probably see individualized feedback as inherent in assessing student work, students notice it, indicating that perhaps it is not the norm. Assessment interactions hold significant potential in connected teaching.

## Asymmetrical Primacy

One additional concept informs the significance of our interactions with students: asymmetrical primacy (Schwartz, 2009). Put simply, interactions and relationships between professors and students tend to hold a different weight or importance for each person, depending on role. I think of this as similar to a doctor's appointment (and even my longer term professional relationship with doctors). When I go to the doctor, I want her full attention, and I want to believe that she cares about me and that my health is important to her. I do not really think about the reality that she is probably seeing 20 other patients that day; I see people in the waiting room so I am aware she has other patients, but from my perspective, they fade into the background, and her appointment with me is vivid; this is how I see her as a doctor. I recall a similar feeling about professors and other mentors who have been important to me. I knew they had other students, but when I was with them online or in person, that was my time. I wanted them to be present and care and to see my academic journey and future as important.

However, when I look at the equation from my perspective as a teacher, I see that meetings and relationships with students are always one of many. Clearly, interactions and relationships differ and have a range of qualities such as energizing or depleting, rewarding or frustrating. Nonetheless, as I learned in my first study, role influences how we view interactions and relationships in terms of primacy. In that study, I interviewed matched pairs of master's faculty and alumni wherein both people said they had a meaningful academic relationship (when the alum was a student). I interviewed the faculty and alumni separately and noticed that while they tended to describe the relationship similarly, sometimes even recalling the same events or qualities, their descriptions diverged.

Recent graduates tended to recall the relationships in greater detail and often described how they were changed by particular interactions or aspects of the relationship. The professors clearly felt strongly connected to these students, but they recalled less detail and often "shifted back and forth in their stories between referring to the specific student and talking more generally about their work with students in the cohort or in the course of a career" (Schwartz, 2009, p. 132).

In the following example, a recent graduate describes the pivotal role his professor played in helping him develop confidence as a leader:

> *In fact, when I did my final presentation, that is another culminating event of the process is we do a—it's a 15- or 20-minute presentation of, well, what did you get out of this—at the end, and that was unbelievable. It really was, because then I really did get a chance to stand flat-footed, and with all the confidence in the world I can share it with anybody, really what this leadership thing was all about, and with the best of them. It really didn't matter—I mean, I've got all the back-up I need. I've got the expert standing right behind me, um, showing the way, and then I can just follow along, but that confidence that I had as a student here is certainly the result of the person who sort of guided me through that entire process. —Jerome* (Schwartz, 2009, p. 133)

The professor also recalled this student's growth and in particular his increased confidence:

*Very rewarding, very affirming of (a) the program and (b) my own efforts, humble as they are, to bring something to the students. I feel very strongly that there are at least two levels of growth in the students. Certainly, there's one in the material, which we share. But there's another one in the personal level, their personal level. And, ah, so it was in that sense that I saw him gain this confidence, that, you just have to rejoice that this is happening. It's not alone with him. There was another couple in that same cohort that I could also have talked about. —Ted* (Schwartz, 2009, p. 133)

The student remembers the moment when he delivered his final presentation, aware of his increased confidence; he recalls this in detail and in relation to his mentor professor. The professor reflects on this meaningful relationship as a manifestation of his ongoing efforts to help students develop; he remembers the student but does so in the context of his teaching career and other students.

> Professors and students are primary or prominent to each other, but the primacy is not symmetrical. A student experiences his mentor professor as a "one," that is to say, the one (or main) mentor in his master's program or the one professor who really saw his potential and pushed him. . . . He sees his graduate school mentor as unique, as holding a singular position in his life. When he talks about his professor, he rarely references other mentors, the relationship is contained within itself. The professor will most likely have a series of notable relationships with students throughout his career. So, to some degree, this student is one of many (one of all students the professor has taught and will teach) and to another degree he is one of a few (one of a few stand out students), however he is not a "one." (Schwartz, 2009, pp. 133–134)

Typically, when we meet with students, the meeting is one of several appointments in a given day or week. However, we are wise to remember that for the student, the meeting or conversation may hold much more significance. For us, the meeting is one of many; for the student, the meeting may be the one—the one that helps them push past a moment of deep doubt or begin to consider a life-changing opportunity.

## The Good News: Students Perceive
## Teaching Time as "Extra Time"

A student sits across from me and 20 minutes into our conversation about her independent study, she says, "I have another question, but I know I'm taking up a lot of your time and you're busy." While I appreciate that the student sees my time as valuable (the opposite of a student who misses an appointment and never apologizes), I am struck that she thinks meeting with her is interrupting my real work or taking me away from something more important. I think to myself, "This is what I'm supposed to be busy with—this is teaching." I thank her and try to affirm that this is what I do, that meeting with students is an important part of teaching and that "my time right now is about you." I have had similar interactions with students I teach online. Wrapping up a one-on-one video call, a student apologizes for "taking so much of my time."

Students hold a variety of expectations regarding time with faculty. Clearly, some students expect us to be available 24/7, but many others still appear to view teaching and learning as something that happens within the walls and time frame of the campus classroom or the parallel structure of the online learning space. These students seem to imagine that a teacher's essential work is manifest during the 90 minutes in front of the class or in structured interactions in the online space, that all teaching is done in the group context, and that any other time we spend with students outside of class or one-on-one online is extra, above and beyond the baseline work of teaching. Even students who expect us to be available on demand may presume we will answer brief questions but still take note when we have extended conversations.

In part, these perceptions likely stem from the fact that many students, regardless of generation, still hold a traditional view of education as a classroom-based process. In addition, these student perceptions, that one-on-one time is "extra time," may also be fueled by the immediacy and speed of communication in the digital era. I generally do not buy the idea that technology has negatively disrupted communication and relationships, but perhaps the digital age has situated us to see individualized interactions as out of the ordinary and thus as having particular meaning.

> *It was meaningful because she was addressing me personally, talking—and I was able to explain where my lack of understanding was, and she was able to fill in the gaps for me and explain the concept that I wasn't correctly understanding. It was meaningful because it was one-on-one tailored to my particular concern as opposed to a lecture in class. —Maggie* (Schwartz & Holloway, 2014, p. 51)

So why does extra time, or time perceived to be beyond the inherent scope of one's job, hold such currency? I get the sense from students I have interviewed that when they think professors choose to spend "extra time" with them, they perceive the professor's interest in them and their work to be authentic rather than simply "part of the job" (Schwartz, 2009). The distinction may not be obvious to us as faculty, as many of us see out-of-class or out-of-LMS (learning management system) conversations as part of teaching; however, it seems to carry weight for some students.

> *I know for me as a student, that's really important to me, to know that this person is, you know, coming here because they really do care about what they're teaching, and it's—you know, it's not a paycheck; it's a little bit more to them, and they're more vested in us.* —Rebecca (Schwartz, 2009, p. 97)

Perhaps from the student perspective, when I explain an assignment to the class, I am just doing my job. Maybe to some degree, what seems to be the instrumental or routine work of teaching appears to be more about the job than the learner. But when I stay after class or schedule a video call to help a student develop her idea for a paper, I am now (from the student perspective), going above and beyond what is expected of me, and thus I must really care about the student's learning. And if the student's learning is important to me, then the student must be important to me, thus the student matters, and this gives the interaction a rich relational quality that is less obvious when I am "just doing my job." So these interactions that students perceive as extra, that are for most of us part of the essential work of teaching, take on a quality of authenticity.

This authenticity adds a layer of meaning and conveys mattering, which RCT suggests is a condition for growth in relation (Fletcher & Ragins, 2007; Jordan, 2010; Miller & Stiver, 1997; Purgason, Avent, Cashwell, Jordan, & Reese, 2016). I talk throughout this book about why I think mattering is essential to learning and focus on this in chapter 9.

In addition, students find interactions meaningful when they believe the interactions are important to the professor (Schwartz & Holloway, 2012, 2014). In studies where this student perception emerged, we did not ask students to imagine what the reported interactions meant to professors; however, unprompted they described and identified as important the interactions they thought were meaningful for faculty. Students' imagining of their work as important to professors again reflects RCT in general and mentoring episodes in particular, both of which indicate that growth-fostering interactions and relationships have a quality of mutuality wherein both people learn, grow, or benefit from the interaction (Edwards & Richards, 2002; Fletcher & Ragins, 2007; Jordan, 2010; Karpouza & Emvalotis, 2018; McMillian-Roberts, 2014; Schwartz & Holloway, 2014). Perhaps a student's experience of mutuality makes the interaction more potent because the student again perceives authenticity—if the student can influence me, I am here as my real self who is open to others and can learn and grow (not as a removed expert who teaches from a distance and thus might be seen as "doing her job" rather than engaging authentically). Conveying to students that we are open to being influenced by them is another element of engaged presence that conveys "I am here with you authentically, and you and your learning matter to me."

## Making Small Moments Bigger: Invite, Be Present, Express Care, and Convey Enthusiasm

What are the qualities that potentially transform single interactions into moments that hold great meaning? Invitation, presence, care, and enthusiasm are intentions that enhance both brief interactions and longer term teaching relationships.

### Inviting Students to Engage

How do we invite students into learning and energize the learning space, particularly when we also face larger class sizes and advising loads; challenges, shifts, and glitches that are part and parcel of teaching online; and increased demands for service? To clarify, student engagement is by no means the full responsibility of the professor. Students have significant responsibility for connecting with faculty. However, given this book's focus, I concentrate on what we as faculty can do to encourage student engagement; however, this focus is not intended to diminish or dismiss students' responsibility to seek and continue engagement with faculty. So how do we invite students to engage?

*Say it again.* After years of offering to meet online or after class with students who have questions or are having difficulty with assignments, we might begin to think that these invitations are hollow. Semester after semester, we offer "If you need help, let me know," and perhaps only a few students respond. Nonetheless, invitation is important, and at least some students are encouraged when faculty offer a direct invitation to connect. Though students may not often respond to our invitations immediately, I suspect that continuing to explicitly invite students to engage keeps the door open and makes contact easier when they finally realize they want or need support or guidance.

*Be the example.* Because we perceive ourselves to be approachable, we may forget that many students face a variety of obstacles as they imagine communicating one-on-one with a teacher. Some students still believe that to ask for help is to show weakness. Again, remember we are all surrounded by the individual achievement narrative. In addition, to whatever degree we are comfortable and confident working in higher education, we are wise to remember that many students enter our learning spaces unsure if they can succeed in the academic environment. First-generation undergraduate students may not have learned how to navigate college, and even graduate students may intuit that they face a new set of unwritten rules about how to engage and achieve on the master's and doctoral levels (Hurtado et al., 2011). We might seem at ease (in some cases despite our own first-generation backgrounds), and this can create distance between teacher and student. Finally, high-achieving students may fear asking for help because they imagine we expect them to be fully competent.

We can challenge these various myths of extreme self-sufficiency and independence-as-success by sharing our own stories. Talking with students about our own struggles and experiences of positive engagement with our teachers sends the message that seeking help or support is a sign of maturity not failure and that learning is a social process.

Inviting students to engage is a routine act of teaching; however, presence, care, and enthusiasm might seem like extras. For some faculty, anything more than teaching content, answering questions, and assessing student learning is either above and beyond the job or nice, but too much to undertake. I propose that real presence with students and small expressions of care and enthusiasm are what power our teaching exchanges and transform them from mere interactions to powerful teaching moments.

### Being Present

> I don't know quite how you describe it, but really seeing the student as an individual and knowing what your background is and what you might bring to this new—this new venture. And certainly it wasn't a rushed conversation. . . . We didn't talk forever, but there certainly—you certainly didn't get the feeling that I—I just need to have this meeting and get it over with. So that was—it was encouraging and supportive. —Natalie (Schwartz & Holloway, 2014, p. 52)

As I review literature for this book, I am struck by the great thinkers who help us understand how presence in connection, even in a singular interaction, promotes growth. From Martin Buber in the mid-twentieth century to Nel Noddings early in the twenty-first century, and many others in the decades between (Daloz, 1999; hooks, 1994; Miller & Stiver, 1997; Palmer, 1998; Parks, 2011; Rogers, 1961), presence is seen as a key ingredient for growth-fostering relationships. Presence conveys a basic level of acceptance, not necessarily agreement or alignment but more basic human receiving, a momentary commitment to *be with* the other. This acceptance communicates mattering or worth that then potentially helps the other feel less alone and also safe enough to share thinking, ask questions, express concerns, and play with ideas. An intellectually safe space (meaning a space where one can try ideas without fear of ridicule or shame and yet feel motivated by challenge and expectations) is foundational for learning and for development.

> *I become a part of the learning process. I take more ownership of what I'm being able to learn because I was able to relate to this professor and I was able to build more of a relationship. I'm able to communicate with the professor and I'm able to engage, and I'm able to learn. I'm able to learn versus just being taught, or just going in—I'm paying you so you can give me information versus no I need to learn and I need to be engaged. —Rebecca* (Schwartz & Holloway, 2014, p. 50)

A clear picture of what it means to be present may be elusive. Several elements combine to create a feeling of being present with another and that another is present with me, including focus and attention, pace (not rushed), listening and feeling heard, steady or increasing energy, and individualized (rather than rote) responses. In Western culture, eye contact and open posture also indicate presence. To be present is to experience mutuality and cocreation. Miller and Stiver (1997) described this phenomenon:

> Through their interaction they have created something new together. Both are enlarged by this creation. Something new now exists, built by both of them. This is what we call "the connection between." It does not belong to one or the other; it belongs to both. Yet each feels it is "hers," as part of her. She contributed to its creation, and it contributed to her, to what she now "is," which is more than she was a few moments before. (p. 38)

Respect is a fundamental element of growth-fostering connections (Edwards & Richards, 2002; Rossiter, 1999; Walker, 2004) and can be an element of presence. RCT scholar Maureen Walker clarifies that respect is not simply something a therapist grants to a client but rather is enacted when one person is open and present with another person (and their own) complexity; a perspective relevant in education as well. Applying her work in the context of teaching, we glean that respect is manifest when we are present with a student and the student's authentic self. "To experience connection is to participate in a relationship that invites exposure, curiosity, and openness to possibility. Simply put, connection provides safety from contempt and humiliation; however it does not promise comfort" (Walker, 2004, p. 9). This conceptualization of respect in presence resonates particularly well with the teaching endeavor wherein we strive to respect the person, even when the work is substandard, when a student plagiarizes, or in other cases where we balance our roles as guides and gatekeepers.

Presence provides a foundation for care and enthusiasm. When a student and I are present with each other (in person or online), I am more likely to sense the student's affective state. I am not suggesting that faculty engage in deep emotional work with students, but sensing whether a student is, for example, anxious or confident will likely help us regulate challenge and support.

## Expressing Care

How does care help a student progress, and why is it important in teaching interactions? Care helps students develop a more mature understanding of learning (Deacon, 2012; Rogers-Shaw & Carr-Chellman, 2018) and create and ask exploratory questions and try new ideas (Brown, 2012; Edwards & Richards, 2002; Hurtado et al., 2011; Piorkowski & Scheurer, 2000; Rossiter, 1999; Schwartz, 2009; Schwartz & Holloway, 2014). Even adult students may enter our courses believing that learning is a solitary endeavor and thus be afraid to ask for help and remain resistant to critical feedback. However, learning to ask for help, engage others in collaborative thinking, and welcome feedback from peers and teachers helps students flourish and positions them as lifelong learners. Piorkowski and Scheurer (2000) found that when students sense that a teacher cares about them and their work, they are more likely to develop skills and the understanding that learning is a social process. In addition, students who are insecure, anxious, intimidated, and afraid of embarrassment or shame are less likely to take intellectual risks (Brown, 2012; Edwards & Richards, 2002; Hurtado et al., 2011; Rossiter, 1999; Schwartz, 2009; Schwartz & Holloway, 2014). Finally, care helps students develop scholar-practitioner identity. "When students could perceive the teacher's caring for them, they developed an image of themselves that was confirmed by the teacher, becoming more confident in themselves, and authoring themselves as better students or prospective teachers" suggest Kim and Schallert (2011, p. 1066), echoing Noddings's (2003) concept of confirmation.

So how do we convey care? Noddings (2003) proposes that care includes engrossment, motivational displacement, and confirmation. Engrossment involves "receiving the other, completely and nonselectively" (p. 176). Mirroring Jordan's (1991, 1997, 2010) explication of empathy, Noddings's engrossment involves not a loss of self to the other but rather a being with the other, being deeply present and willing to share one's "motive power" in the other's service. "My motivational energies are flowing toward him and, perhaps, toward his ends" (Noddings, 2003, p. 17). And as noted previously, this can all lead to confirmation—teacher and student see each other's better selves, and that glimpse provides the next step forward, the boost of energy as noted in RCT, and the motivation for more teaching and learning.

Rossiter (1999) and Deacon (2012) help transfer Noddings's work into practice. Rossiter (1999), in a study with adult learners, identified the following components of caring: "to be noticed, to be understood, to have one's concerns be a priority for another, to be shown one's best self, to value the one caring, to trust and receive, and to be respected" (pp. 209–210). The following student describes care as a form of connection, noting that one professor in particular helped her return after an extended absence:

> *Really it just showed that she cared. I've been back to school for a week and none of my other professors went to the length that she did to make sure that my adjustment back to school was a good one, so I would say she probably went above and beyond compared to my other professors. —Dawn* (Schwartz & Holloway, 2014, p. 53)

While Rossiter's (1999) components of care are applicable in the campus classroom and online, Deacon (2012) provides strategies for creating a context of care specifically online. She encourages faculty to intentionally design their online learning spaces (rather than using default structures that might not suit the course or the students), anticipate that students (even those who are fluent in the digital realm) may have anxiety about learning online, and build a sense of community via online discussion spaces.

Teaching from a relational perspective inherently calls on us to "study the conditions that make it possible for caring relations to flourish" (Noddings, 2003, p. xiv). While our intention may be to teach from a place of care, this approach also comes with challenges. We encounter students who seem to need more than we can (or feel is appropriate to) provide and students with whom we have difficulty connecting.

In addition, students may expect us to be available and care 24/7. For those who teach online or who use online spaces in combination with campus classrooms, we may feel responsibility to manage (care for) the online learning space (Rose & Adams, 2014), including the technology that drives it. Few faculty intended to be technologists, and yet many of us are at least somewhat involved in fielding inquiries when something does not work in the online learning space. Rose and Adams suggest that the immediacy of the digital world has made students less likely to try to solve their own academic dilemmas and that they are quicker to ask for help. Many faculty who teach online face a relentless demand for immediate responses to e-mails and other inquires, and this creates a tension between caring for students and caring for self (Rose & Adams, 2014).

## Enthusiasm

Students notice when we are enthusiastic about course content, our disciplines, our research, and of course their ideas and work.

> *Well, it's just—uh, excitement breeds excitement. I mean, when you begin to understand something you want more understanding . . . there's nothing more attractive to me than—you know, and this is the way I feel about teaching right now is I have a glimpse of who I could be as a teacher—I haven't figured out how to get there yet, and so there's sort of this—this trek of challenge of—you know, and in watching him talk and discuss, it was like whoa, I only—like that's the tip of the iceberg, you know, like I know there's more. I know there's bigger—I know there's deeper, so you know, it just triggered this wanting to know more. —Maria* (Schwartz, 2009, p. 105)

Much like care, enthusiasm conveys to students that they and their thinking matter to us (Schwartz, 2009, 2013; Schwartz & Holloway, 2014). Our excitement conveys the social nature of learning proposed by Piorkowski and Scheurer (2000) as we model the power of collaboration to stretch our thinking beyond what any of us can do individually. Enthusiasm can also reassure a student who is struggling with imposter syndrome or other forms of insecurity, or fear of failure. Showing enthusiasm for a student's idea conveys "you can do this" even more convincingly than saying "you can do this." And like care, our enthusiasm also encourages students to explore ideas, take intellectual risks, and begin to see themselves as cocreators of knowledge and ideas regarding application, in turn reinforcing their motivation. Perhaps enthusiasm is a potential fuel for the motivation transfer described by Noddings (2003). When a student shares an idea and I respond with enthusiasm, she takes in that excitement and leaves more motivated for the project; my enthusiasm transfers to her, and she leaves the interaction with increased motivation.

For some faculty, enthusiasm is inherent in teaching. For others, enthusiasm or excitement might seem risky or even devaluing of the seriousness of education (hooks, 1994). Excitement in the teaching space may be considered transgressive, as it requires professors to see and begin to know students as individuals and to be flexible in their teaching (hooks, 1994). Excitement that fuels teaching and learning is about more than ideas (hooks, 1994); it is relational, and it is cocreated: "As a classroom community, our capacity to generate excitement is deeply affected by our interest in one another, in hearing one another's voices, in recognizing one another's presence. . . . To begin, the professor must genuinely value everyone's presence" (hooks, 1994, p. 8). Excitement emerges from a relational place. "Although it may seem that when we enter the lecture hall we are 'teaching a class,' always it is individuals who are learning" (Daloz, 1999, p. xix).

Enthusiasm and excitement are elements and manifestations of the zest that Miller and Stiver (1997) described. They suggested we are energized by connection because in connection we feel alive, a sense of vitality. Translated to teaching and learning, I propose that enthusiasm and excitement reaffirm us in our identities as professor and student, and this energizes us and fuels the teaching and learning process. When a student is excited about a connection he sees between course content and a situation at work, and I respond, we not only increase understanding but also affirm the importance of the concept and validate each other. The student has chosen to be a learner, and I have chosen to be a teacher, and we are both in this moment flourishing in these roles (of course there are times when I learn from him, so in fact the teaching and learning are fluid).

We also experience those "aha!" moments alone, gaining insight from a reading or from the thinking that happens as we write, but I suggest that there is a particular spark that happens when we engage in learning moments with another, when our enthusiasm for content and new understanding meets in a relational moment. Energy as manifest in relational interactions connects closely with enthusiasm as it emerged in teaching research (Daloz, 1999; Schwartz & Holloway, 2014). Like energy and zest as described by Miller and Stiver (1997), enthusiasm in teaching and learning increases vitality. Thus, I suggest that enthusiasm can be particularly generative for us as faculty. While expressing care for a student might feel important but also at times draining, enthusiasm, at least in the moment and often for at least a short time after the interaction, increases our own energy.

As noted throughout this chapter, teaching with enthusiasm and care can be a demanding endeavor. In the next chapter, we explore boundaries in connected teaching.

# 3

# "CAN I TEXT YOU?"

## Adjusting and Maintaining
## Boundaries in the Digital Age

Teaching has always involved questions regarding interpersonal boundaries with students. Those of us who teach adults may encounter students in community, professional, and social settings and may find ourselves in comparable life stages with our students (e.g., raising children, caring for aging parents). Those who teach 18- to 22-year-olds may face fewer of these dynamics but still confront decisions regarding matters such as accessibility, self-disclosure, and response time. Furthermore, the challenges and dilemmas we face have shifted as the 24/7 digital world and millennial expectations raise new questions regarding availability, flexibility, privacy, and related topics.

I begin this exploration of boundaries with an overview—clarifying the faculty role, defining boundaries, and considering identity and power. Next, I discuss three contextual elements of the digital age: discomfort with new technology, shifting constructs of time, and the changing nature of self-disclosure. In the final section, I offer a connected teaching approach to boundaries including reflection, intention, and relational and role clarity.

## Overview

Throughout this chapter, I encourage readers to examine reflexive boundary constructs and to view boundaries as a place of growth and productivity rather than restriction and separation (Jordan, 2010). Concurrently, we must be clear on our role as teachers. I write from a relational perspective and am committed to reducing hierarchy, and yet I also remain fully aware that in my relationships with students, I hold a different role and set of responsibilities than they do. As someone who evaluates student work, I hold more power than the student, and thus the student is vulnerable in the relationship (Jordan, 2010; Schwartz, 2011; Tom, 1997). Moreover, I am responsible for the learning space and relationship; I must seek to create learning spaces and relationships that balance challenge and support and to prioritize student learning and development. Students do not assume these same responsibilities in the learning context and in our relationship.

At the same time, we are two people in a relationship. Most likely, both of us get some of our needs met. This is natural in meaningful human interaction and is a sign of the potential mutuality in teaching and learning (Tom, 1997). Remaining conscious that teaching meets some of our needs (e.g., connection, respect, a sense of contribution, a sense of mattering to others) positions us to prevent these needs from driving our interactions, shaping our relationships, or otherwise influencing us as teachers. "Mutuality depends on shared vulnerability and openness to change, but it does not indicate sameness of role or symmetry in disclosure" (Jordan, 2010, p. 56). Professors who work close to the boundaries while also remaining faithful to their teaching responsibilities are keenly aware of their evaluative responsibilities; clearly articulate the faculty role; and, despite multiple roles and variations on the teaching relationship (such as mentor, adviser, colleague), remain "a teacher in the life of a student" (Schwartz, 2011, p. 367).

## Boundaries Defined

In the popular culture view of teaching, the notion of interpersonal boundaries serves to remind students and professors they should not engage in romantic or sexual relationships. These relationships are frequently prohibited by institutional policy, such as those at Brandeis University (Brandeis University, 2012), University of Pittsburgh (Faculty-Student Relationships, n.d.), University of Texas (Consensual Relationships, 2017), and Stanford University (1.7.2 Consensual Sexual or Romantic Relationships, 2017). The importance of refraining from such relationships wherein there is a power imbalance and significant risk of favoritism, manipulation, and other emotional disruption to the learning endeavor cannot be overstated. At the same time, I believe most faculty are far more challenged by routine and frequent dilemmas such as availability and self-disclosure. As a concept, boundaries provide a guide for professional relationships (Barnett, 2008), particularly in cases where there is a power imbalance.

Boundaries are often conceptualized as protection against wrongdoing and thus may seem fixed. However, boundaries are a social construct, shaped by aspects of identity such as culture, social class, and generation. For example, Japanese students studying in U.S.-based programs might be reluctant to approach a professor they do not know well. This would be consistent with Eastern cultures wherein interactions tend to be guided by degree of familiarity and a high regard for authority (Yamashita & Schwartz, 2012). American-born faculty may misinterpret this dynamic with Japanese students as indifference. In this example, both students and professors are acting in accordance with their perceptions of appropriateness, and still their assumptions about the other's motivations may be incorrect. Clearly, a student and teacher who both think they are acting appropriately may find their connection and communication disrupted by conflicting views of boundaries.

Long-standing views of the role of boundaries suggest they "may be rigidly enforced, crossed, or violated" (Barnett, 2008, pp. 5–6). From Barnett's perspective, boundary crossings are not definitively unethical or violating and in fact may be typical in many teaching relationships wherein teacher and student work closely, share appropriate self-disclosure, attend a professional conference together, or exchange hugs at graduation. A focus on boundaries as fixed and prescriptive for what we cannot do as teachers (e.g., self-disclose or share our cell phone number) positions us to think that at any moment, someone in the relationship is about to break a rule, violate the relationship, or take advantage of the other. This defensive stance leaves us in a protective position and diminishes the possibility of boundaries as complex and evolving.

A fixed view may also lead to excessive distance or denial. Fearful of what they imagine to be a slippery slope regarding power and boundaries (regarding anything from a friendly student to one who asks for a deadline extension), some faculty enact a distance response (Tom, 1997), seeking to maintain what they imagine is a necessary hierarchy between teachers and students. This response can diminish the potential for creative intellectual exchange (Barnett, 2008; Schwartz, 2011; Tom, 1997); "such a frame reduces both faculty members and students to cardboard caricatures attempting to create a relationship" (Tom, 1997, p. 9). In addition, this distancing does not allow students to learn how to navigate the complexities of professional relationships (Tom, 1997) or to critique or challenge power (hooks, 1994; Tom, 1997). Moreover, capitalizing on the distance available in a hierarchical relationship creates the potential for misuse of power and "increases the privilege associated with the teacher's role through the creation of a kind of mystique" (Tom, 1997, p. 9).

While some faculty exploit the distance afforded by the teaching role, others deny the differences between the teacher and student roles, which is also inherently problematic (Tom, 1997). Teachers wishing to reduce the power differential with students may seek to refute or even relinquish their power. Adult educators might be particularly tempted to suggest that everyone in the learning space (students and teachers alike) are adults and thus co-learners and that the teaching role is backgrounded or disappears. This stance does a disservice to students because if we are assessing student work (as well as approving course changes, writing letters of recommendation, and holding other forms of influence over students' short- and long-term futures), we hold power in the relationship. To refute this is to ask students to live in a space of denial wherein they know we hold power but are to act as if we do not (Robertson, 2005; Tom, 1997). Of deeper concern, when we obfuscate the existing power differential, we potentially deny students the ability to put their needs before ours. If a student feels her obligation to support her professor is equal to her right to ask the professor for help with a paper, she may not ask for help and is no longer getting what is rightfully hers, that is, support for her learning.

Finally, a faculty member who seeks to relinquish power or deny the power differential also surrenders her responsibility to maintain a productive learning space (Buck, Mast, Latta, & Kaftan, 2009; Holloway & Alexandre, 2012; Tom, 1997). For example, if one student keeps interrupting another student, the professor has a responsibility to intervene. The sometimes-difficult work of shaping and maintaining the learning space is central in the teaching role, and forfeiting this responsibility has the potential to diminish the student experience and learning.

Relational-Cultural Theory (RCT) helps us see beyond a fixed view that focuses on distance or denial. "RCT sees the boundary as a place of meeting, learning, differentiation, and exchange" (Jordan, 2010, p. 14). The RCT stance does not diminish the importance of boundaries; however, it calls on us to begin to consider the concept as *role* boundaries rather than *interpersonal* boundaries:

> Some role boundaries . . . are inevitable and desirable as they help protect against abuse of power. Role boundaries describe expectations in professionally defined situations, and these expectations support safety and growth. Professors have the responsibility to support the student's role as well as to attend to their own clarity and professional standards. Effective boundaries help us maintain differentiation, but do not increase separation. (Jordan & Schwartz, 2018, p. 30)

This reimagining pushes us to see boundaries as a commitment to professionalism and care for students without inherently creating distance in the teaching and learning relationship. Clearly, there are students who seek to engage relationally beyond what is appropriate in the context of a power-differentiated relationship. In these cases, faculty may need to establish greater clarity regarding roles. However, rather than starting from a place of establishing distance, RCT invites us to move closer to the boundaries and view them as powerful learning spaces.

Drawing on Jordan's (2010) paradigm-shifting work, I propose we approach boundaries as an opportunity to "learn and become more relationally competent rather than by a need to impose limits or control" (p. 56). For example, by seeking to understand the generationally based assumptions that our students make, we expand our awareness of how we have been shaped by our own generational context. Likewise, I have heard colleagues, when discussing the impact of generational differences among teachers and students, declare the dialogue was useful in understanding not only students but also their own teenagers. In these ways, approaching boundaries as a learning space rather than a control space makes us better teachers and enhances our learning. This RCT view and a deeper understanding of cultural and generational shifts situate us to explore our position with greater intention and clarity.

### *When Students Hold Identity Power and Challenge Our Position*

I write this chapter aware that I do so as a white woman who teaches at a women-centered university where typically there are fewer than 5 men in a class of 18 to 20 students. As a white woman, I do not typically have the experience that many colleagues of color face wherein white students question (implicitly or explicitly) their intellect, qualifications, or political agenda (Gutiérrez y Muhs, Niemann, González, & Harris, 2012; hooks, 1994; Hua, 2018; Johnson-Bailey, 2015; Nair, 2018; Shockley, 2013). So, as I write this chapter, I do so from a place where I rarely deal with students who challenge my credibility because of my identity, and I believe this allows me to focus on moving toward the boundaries. Were I to deal regularly with students who hold more privilege than I do, particularly regarding race and gender, I would probably have started this chapter by discussing how one maintains a boundary or works close to the boundary when students begin the relationship with a sense of superiority.

Juanita Johnson-Bailey (2015) recalls teaching a doctoral course on writing for publication; attempting to be transparent about her own writing and publication process and experiences, she shared a selection of her electronic document folders, allowing students to follow an article from "conception to completion" (p. 44):

There was one woman student who, despite my publication history, could not believe I had done the work. So during various course discussions, she offered the following comments as part of her forward assault: (a) Your co-authors have been very generous in giving you first author position on publications so you could establish a research record; (b) I would have been ashamed to send this first draft to a journal; and (c) I'm sure it must be easier for you to get published since you are a Black woman writing mostly about race. (p. 44)

The student made these comments in class in front of other students. Johnson-Bailey addressed them via a range of strategies, including direct examples and humor: "Although I was the professor and the de facto authority in the classroom, possessing the knowledge and expertise to write and publish, it was the student who demanded that I justify and defend my right to teach her" (Johnson-Bailey, 2015, p. 44). Clearly one's sociocultural identity sets a context regarding how one will be received by students, and this sets a context for considering boundaries.

## The Changing Context: Technology, Time, and Self-Disclosure

Technology and resulting cultural shifts have changed the environment in which we navigate role boundaries with students. In this section, I discuss technology as a source of stress, a shaper of time, and a force that has blurred distinctions between professional and personal context.

### *Damn the VCR: Fear and Frustration in the Land of Computing*

Technology is "anything that isn't around when you're born" (Alan Kay, cited in Frand, 2000, p. 13). Devices driven by the microchip have changed the ways we work, play, teach, and learn. These devices have reshaped not only how we do but also how we think. When we consider the generations represented among faculty and students, we see an obvious range of experiences with technology and thus mind-sets about and comfort with devices and apps. While for many faculty, technology is a source of stress, Frand (2000) reminds us that for many students, "computers aren't technology" (p. 16); they simply are.

I think the VCR scarred a generation. A device that promised to change how we watched television was difficult if not seemingly impossible for many people to program, and so many developed anticipatory fear and frustration over learning new electronic equipment. Then along came the personal computer, which often froze or crashed, and the early word processing programs in which one wrong move could result in losing a document and hours of work. This intensified the fear of failure and the sheer frustration of trying new forms of technology. Even though today's devices and apps are by many standards easier to use and harder to crash, I believe those early experiences remain in the background as faculty are pushed to work with new learning management systems, apps within those systems, and other technology-driven modes of communication with students. This discomfort (conscious or not) may add another layer of stress as we try to manage the deeper technology-driven shifts regarding boundaries.

## *Rethinking Time: Open All Night*

For those of us raised in a precomputing or pre-pervasive-computing world, time itself may have, for much of our lives, indicated particular boundaries. Many of us who teach grew up in a time when you did not contact your professor outside of office hours, and thus you would never have expected the answer to a question in the evening or over the weekend. In the current world of teaching, we often encounter students who expect an immediate response to a question or paper submitted online. We could easily dismiss this expectation as insensitive or entitled. While I do not suggest that we need to feel obligated to respond to students immediately, I propose that understanding their mind-set may help us avoid annoyance and model or teach a respectful approach to boundaries in the digital age.

As I write this chapter, I realize I straddle two different sets of expectations regarding time and response. To some degree, I do not expect people to answer work e-mail in the evening or on weekends. This perspective was shaped by my experience in childhood and young adulthood. When I was growing up, my parents worked daytime weekday schedules and did not bring work home. Moreover, there was not much one could do in the late evening or beyond. You would not call someone's house after a certain hour. Aside from *Saturday Night Live*, there was not much to see on pre-cable TV after about 11:00 p.m. Even after my cohort reached driving age, virtually nothing in my rural area was open after midevening. In retrospect, my world sort of closed for business after about 9:00 p.m. on weeknights and midnight on weekends.

At the same time, I realize that in some cases, I am surprised when a colleague does not respond quickly, even in the evening or over a weekend. Reflecting, I realize I hold a somewhat random set of assumptions, that people who hold higher positions in my work life (e.g., provost or president) and support staff, respond only during regular work hours. As I interrogate this, I realize I only imagine them responding to e-mail from their offices (so I guess I do not expect them to be working when they are not in their offices—in many cases, a faulty assumption). But I expect evening and weekend responses from peer colleagues (whom I imagine work from home and read e-mail on their phones as I do). Reflecting more intentionally, I share this to suggest that my assumptions about time and response are ultimately based on my rather arbitrary imaging about who does work where and on what devices. I imagine the provost reads mail on her phone, and I know a few peer colleagues who do not tend to answer e-mail on weekends. While I can imagine both a world that shuts down in the evening and over weekends and a world structured around immediate response, I suspect many of our incoming students know only an immediate-response world.

Teens today can do significantly more 24/7 than I could at their age. They can text; chat; comment on Snapchat, Twitter, Facebook, and other social media; shop online; stream music, shows, and movies; and search and find seemingly endless information—all without leaving home and often from the privacy of their own room via cellphone, tablet, or laptop (if they have their own room, own such devices, and have Internet access—not necessarily true for young people from all socioeconomic backgrounds). And of course, they can not only initiate these activities but also receive an immediate response from friends, family, or customer support. So when millennial students expect an immediate response, they may not be feeling entitled (at least not in the pejorative sense); they may simply and tacitly expect interaction to be immediate. While some of us might ask, "How can you expect me to respond immediately or on an evening or weekend?" they might be thinking, "Why aren't you answering; is your phone broken?"

Again, this is not to say we should feel obligated to be available to students all the time but rather to say that it is useful to understand a mind-set common among students of this generation. Of note, this expectation is not limited to millennials; indeed, many of us, as we become accustomed to 24/7 customer service and next-day delivery, also increasingly expect immediate responses as we navigate daily life.

### Self-Disclosure and Context Collapse

Another dynamic in play for those of us who grew up before pervasive computing is the belief that we can shape our self-presentation based on the situation (I bring a slightly different self to the classroom than I do to lunch with a friend) and that we can keep various domains (work, family, friends, politics) separate. Who we are talking with and the location of the interaction influence our split-second assessment of what we wish to share and how we will present (Goffman, 1959; Marwick & boyd, 2010; Vitak, 2012). However, "social media technologies collapse multiple audiences into single contexts, making it difficult for people to use the same techniques online that they do to handle multiplicity in face-to-face conversations" (Marwick & boyd, 2010, p. 1). In addition, disclosure in social media spaces reach not only our intended audiences but also unintended audiences (Marwick & boyd, 2010; Vitak, 2012). Increasing numbers of students have come of age amidst collapsed contexts wherein they have not seen distinctions in how one might interact differently with people in different settings (Marwick & boyd, 2010; Vitak, 2012). So while some professors may be swimming upstream trying to compartmentalize life in a way that is increasingly difficult in a digital world, students (and perhaps younger faculty) may not even grasp the distinctions between personal and professional.

To some degree, context collapse may have upsides (boyd, 2002; Marwick & boyd, 2010; Sugimoto, Hank, Bowman, & Pomerantz, 2015). For example, students find faculty more trustworthy and approachable when they see us as multifaceted human beings rather than simply people whose job is teaching (Brookfield, 2006; Schwartz & Holloway, 2012, 2014). In addition, students may more readily receive and integrate informal feedback and formal assessment when they have what they perceive to be a personal connection with a professor (Brookfield, 2017; Schwartz & Holloway, 2012). So the ways in which social media and digital age communication allow students to see us as authentic and complex rather than one-dimensional is not inherently bad. Further, engagement in social networking sites such as LinkedIn can help students and faculty develop additional social capital, for example, an expanded network for internship and job searches (Vitak, 2012). Yet for many faculty, navigating social media and LMS spaces is an ongoing and shifting boundary-related challenge. Context collapse shapes us and our students as we navigate decisions regarding self-disclosure, availability, response time, and overall presentation of self, from the photos we share to the profile descriptions we craft for various platforms.

*Broadcasting the personal.* In addition to context collapse, the digital era has changed the sharing and permanence of interpersonal interactions, which are now often recorded, broadcast, and then made available beyond one's control (Marwick & boyd, 2010). For example, a student secretly records a professor in class and shares the video on YouTube, or a teacher comments on an alum's Facebook post, forgetting that the alum is also connected with current students who may see the post. University policies, privacy settings, and intention regarding friend requests and sharing may provide faculty and students with some degree of control in the digital domain; however, everything from lack of understanding or disregard for policies and privacy settings to the one-button broadcast potential and archival quality of anything shared online can make managing boundaries seem markedly different from the way it was in the days when all student faculty interactions happened in the classroom, office, or margins of a printed paper.

*Multiple relationships then and now.* With the emergence of context collapse, discussions regarding multiple relationships take on new complexity and urgency. Prior to the digital age, multiple relationships typically developed out of at least some degree of intention. Barnett (2008) defines *multiple relationships* as "the practice of engaging in additional relationships with another individual in addition to the primary professional relationship" (p. 7). A professor who invites one of her students to housesit on weekends is engaging in multiple relationships, as are a professor and student who decide to start a business together while the student is still in school. Barnett (2008) notes that multiple relationships are not inherently unethical but that the fundamentally divergent roles and goals may lead to exploitation or harm. At the same time, Barnett (2008) acknowledges that many faculty engage in multiple roles within a relationship, such as course teacher, adviser, and mentor. There is less potential for harm in multiple role situations because these roles typically fall under the same professional umbrella and thus there is a consistency to the perimeters of the roles and desired outcomes.

Context collapse in the digital world and in social media spaces in particular can lead to unintended multiple relationship scenarios. When we share information, photos, and videos in online social spaces, they can be seen instantly by people from many parts of our lives (a distinction relevant for those who still see various social circles as differentiated). Regardless of our imagined or intended audience, our now-shared material is available and open for interpretation by known and unknown recipients (Marwick & boyd, 2010; Sugimoto et al., 2015). Exploring multiple relationships in the campus context, Barnett (2008) suggests setting (location) as one of the elements that helps us determine whether a boundary crossing would become a violation. Context collapse largely removes setting as a guiding element in navigating disclosure and multiple relationships, so while some faculty may imagine they can use setting as a reference point, the online world largely negates setting as context.

Clearly, faculty vary in their approaches to social media. Some faculty still decline to engage in social media (beyond the social world of a university LMS). On the other end of the spectrum are those who integrate spaces like Facebook and Twitter with their teaching or who accept friend requests from current students. There are professionals who do not attend to privacy settings and others who are vigilant. Teachers who have largely avoided social media are less likely to face related boundary-blurring moments (though could still get caught up in such an experience if a student chooses to share something related to the professor online). For the rest of us, decisions regarding online personas; participation in social media spaces; and what, where, and when to post and share remain ongoing challenges and decision points.

## Boundaries: A Connected Teaching Approach

As noted previously, connected teaching is typically a stance and a way of being rather than a set of steps. However, regarding boundaries, I offer concrete strategies to more deeply self-reflect and act with greater awareness. In the following section, I consider reflection, intention, and relational and role clarity as strategies for a connected teaching approach to boundaries.

### *Reflection*

Reflecting on power, reflexive boundaries, and the assumptions we hold about our students helps us gain clarity regarding our tacit understandings of boundaries.

First, understanding the power we hold as teachers, our views regarding that power, and our related blind spots is fundamental in examining our approach to boundaries in the teaching context. In chapter 6, we explore power as a fundamental energy in relationships (Walker, 2002b), the connection between power and identity, and approaches to help us work with greater intention regarding position and other forms of power in the teaching relationship.

A second element of this reflection is to identify and interrogate reflexive or default boundaries. Many faculty tend to approach teaching as we were taught (Dunn-Haley & Zanzucchi, 2012), and this may include the lines we draw regarding availability and self-disclosure. As noted earlier in this chapter, changes in technology and generational expectations call on us to reconsider previously held boundary assumptions. "Although deeper reflection may lead us to shift some boundaries, we may hold fast to others. The point of examining reflexive boundaries is not always to alter them but to ensure we are acting with clarity and intention" (Schwartz, 2012c, p. 100).

For example, when I began teaching adult students, I decided to share my cell phone number, knowing that students often have questions when I am not in my office. Students have not abused this level of access and rarely call or text in the evening or on weekends. While sharing my cell number is an example of *expanding* the boundary, I have shifted in the other direction regarding Facebook. Initially, I taught in a small master's program and at that point felt comfortable accepting friend requests from current students. When I transitioned to a larger graduate program with slightly different dynamics between students and faculty, I decided for a variety of reasons to decline friend requests from current students and from alumni as well. Instead I encourage students and alumni to connect with me on LinkedIn. In either case I could have made snap decisions about what felt appropriate, but instead I examined my assumptions and logic before deciding whether (and possibly how) to shift.

The following questions help us interrogate reflexive boundaries:

1. What boundaries have I set reflexively?
2. What assumptions underlie those boundaries?
3. Does setting these boundaries contribute to students' growth and development?
4. Do these assumptions still ring true or make sense in the current context?
5. Would adjusting these boundaries disrupt my self care?

As we begin to reflect on instinctive boundaries, our choices often seem logical and even self-evident. However, further exploration may help us realize some of our assumptions are no longer valid.

A third element of this reflection is to seek to uncover the assumptions we make about students and their motivations. As noted earlier in this chapter, a student who seems overly demanding, expecting an immediate response to an e-mail may seem entitled, but for a millennial student, there may be no reference point that allows him to expect otherwise. Also, as noted previously, this does not mean we have an obligation to respond immediately but rather to understand the student's context so we do not misattribute their motivations, which can then trigger our own resentment or hostility.

### Intention

We approach boundaries with greater intention by calling on the mindful pause, engaging in explicit communication, and offering transparency.

*The mindful pause.* Allison Tom (1997), in what I consider one of the most astute and helpful pieces written about boundaries in adult learning, proposes the *deliberate relationship* as a framework for thinking about teaching as a relational practice:

> In the deliberate relationship, there is a pause between the experience of an impulse and its expression. In that pause, however brief, we interrogate the impulse: Does it serve the long-term obligations of the relationship? If the answer is No, we refrain. In this way, the thoughts and feelings expressed in the deliberate relationship are both genuine and controlled. Learning to be deliberate in relationship requires learning to pause, to ask, and then to act responsibly. (Tom, 1997, p. 12)

As noted earlier in this chapter and initially by Tom (1997), some of our needs are met in our interactions and relationships with students. For example, we feel we contribute to our discipline or profession as we develop novice practitioners. We experience the joy of seeing a student grow from insecure to confident, believing we have helped the student develop. And when we share our stories, we provide powerful examples of a theory in practice or we affirm that even seemingly successful professors faced obstacles as students.

However, self-disclosure can also become more about us than our students, more about serving our needs than theirs, and this is the tipping point. For example, teaching a career development course to counseling students, I search for a story that will illustrate the concept of the psychological contract in the workplace. I recall a relevant experience with a supervisor at another institution. If I would have shared that story with students immediately after the conflict, I probably would have been emotionally raw; students would likely have sensed my frustration and may have felt uncomfortable or even that they should try to encourage or comfort me. This would have been an example of a self-disclosure boundary violation, because in sharing the story, my needs would likely have superseded the students' role as learners. However, in telling this story years later, when I no longer felt upset about the experience, my self-disclosure served students as it helped them understand the concept.

Self-disclosure of humorous stories in the classroom provides an additional example. Graham's (2010) research has helped me become more intentional about my use of humor in teaching. Graham explored the subjective experience of humor-producers in the workplace and identified several appropriate reasons why professionals use humor, including to connect with colleagues, boost morale, and refocus attention in meetings. Her findings moved me to consider that moment when I am about to make (what I think is) a funny comment in class or in meetings with students. I realized that while I sometimes try to be funny for the kinds of positive reasons Graham identified (e.g., to build rapport or garner students' attention), I also simply get a boost when students laugh at my jokes, and I should recognize this impetus as well. After reflecting on this moment of decision and seeing the range of possible motivations, I now pause briefly when I feel inclined to try to be funny and ask myself whether I simply desire to be seen favorably among students, will humor potentially accomplish something else in this moment, or even will humor interrupt what is otherwise a good engaged dialogue in the classroom. When I am as clear as I can be that my humor will not interrupt a good learning moment and is about trying to connect or energize the space (rather than being liked), then I feel free to inject humor.

These deliberations might sound laborious, but in fact once our motives and intentions are clear, we process these moments quickly. The mindful pause is one of the most important maneuvers in connected teaching. The pause is helpful not only regarding self-disclosure and humor but also in setting parameters regarding availability, response time, social media, and possible engagement in multiple relationships.

*Explicit communication.* Communicating with greater specificity and clarity positions us to work closer to the boundaries while also maintaining professionalism and managing students' expectations (Booth & Schwartz, 2012; McEwan, 2012; Schwartz, 2012c). For example, clarify expectations with students regarding forums for communication (e-mail, phone, text, instant message, office meetings). In addition, ask students to indicate their preference and then negotiate that given your preferences. For example, I tell students that while I am happy to answer brief questions via text, I will move to e-mail for longer exchanges. And if the question requires additional back-and-forth, I might suggest a phone call. I share with students that these preferences help me be efficient. Many students prefer text, so even though texting is not my ideal forum, I accommodate it up to the point at which I find it less efficient. In addition to clarifying modes of communication, I try to provide students with my expected response time so they know how quickly I will answer e-mails, return papers, and respond to other inquiries.

Student requests for support beyond our primary teaching or advising relationship provide another example. When students ask me to provide additional guidance or mentoring, I initiate a conversation about how we will work together. For example, students occasionally ask me to consult on a research project for another class (when they anticipate that my subject-matter knowledge could be helpful). First, I clarify my role as supportive and confirm the course teacher is the final authority regarding the assignment. Second, when students seek extra help, I am clear they should initiate all meetings; I will not pursue them, as I want the extra work to be driven by their motivation.

*Transparency.* Finally, transparency serves as an additional strategy for those wishing to manage boundaries from a connected teaching perspective. Transparency regarding self-disclosure, availability, and other boundary-related decisions helps reduce the power differential while allowing us to remain in our teaching roles. By sharing our thinking, we help students learn to manage boundary questions in the workplace. For example, when we describe our rationale for self-disclosure, we may help students think more deeply about their choices in professional relationships. Likewise, as noted earlier in this chapter, when we communicate our availability explicitly, we may help millennial students understand that availability in the workplace is not 24/7.

## *Relational Clarity*

As discussed in chapter 1, relational clarity guides effective relationships and fuels identity development and relational competence. Relational clarity is also an important element of a connected teaching approach to boundaries.

How can we develop greater relational clarity? First, reflect on previous situations in which you might not have maintained relational clarity. Return to the framework in chapter 1 for prompts to reflect on the interaction. For example, how would you describe the connection or disconnection you felt with the student? At what point might you have lost clarity regarding what was the student's experience and what was yours? If helpful, review these situations with a trusted colleague.

Second, adopt a short list of guiding questions to ask yourself if you sense you may be losing clarity in an interaction or relationship with a student. Suggested guiding questions include the following:

1. At times, do I feel as if I am having this experience, when in fact it is the student's experience?
2. Did the emotion (e.g., anger, anxiety, frustration, sadness) originate with the student or me?
3. Are my emotions more heightened than the student's?
4. Do I find myself preoccupied about the student's experience or problem when I am off campus or away from the computer?
5. Are my emotions (relating to the student's situation) overwhelming?

These questions can become part of the mindful pause we practice when engaging with students. As noted before, this processing may appear cumbersome, but once this process is integrated, we can use these questions to quickly clarify our experience.

As we will see in remaining chapters, clarity and intention regarding boundaries serves as a foundation for connected teaching approaches to assessment, dealing with disruption, and a range of emotional challenges we face in the classroom and online.

# 4

# ASSESSMENT AS RELATIONAL PRACTICE

## Increasing Receptivity and Motivation Through Connected Teaching

*We face this dual role, I think, of being both mentors and guides and at the same time, we are still academic gatekeepers, whether it's a master's program or undergraduate program or PhD program. . . . So how do we mesh these two roles of being, on the one hand, what I'm calling the academic gatekeeper or the academic approver, if you want, with that of being a guide and a mentor and of being emotionally involved with students? To me, that's the crux of what we're talking about. And it's never easy—we just do it, one student at a time.*
—Sandra (Schwartz & Holloway, 2017, p. 51)

Through relationship we seek to regulate challenge and support, and at the same time, we are gatekeepers for our disciplines and professions. In relationship, we seek to increase student receptivity to feedback and help students reach toward clarity; critical thinking; and, for those who already excel, greater challenge. In addition, we come to assessment interactions with our identities, emotional makeup, and current emotional state, as do our students; "assessment is not simply a one-way act in which teachers deliver feedback to students, but rather an exchange between educators and learners involving relational dynamics, emotion, and degrees of receptivity" (Schwartz, 2017, p. 6).

In this chapter, I consider the meaning that assessment may hold for students and faculty and provide examples of assessment interactions in which relational elements strengthen or detract from the potential for learning. From this foundation, we explore a connected teaching approach to increasing student receptivity to feedback and ultimately helping students reach higher. First, a word about rigor.

## Rigor, Connection, and the Evaluator Paradox

Conventional wisdom suggests assessment requires distance and objectivity, which may seem incompatible with connected teaching. I suggest that instead of seeking relational distance from students, we return to the idea of role clarity, which positions us to review student work fairly and rigorously without needing to disconnect from the relationship. This clarity situates us to manage the tension inherent in the teaching role, that we are both "helper and judge" (Robertson, 2001b). We ask students to take risks—to ask questions, share their thinking, perhaps even challenge our assumptions or claims. And all the while, students know eventually we will assess their work, often assigning grades. In addition, we control access, and that gives us power; students may ask us to lobby for their entrance into a closed course or to write a letter of recommendation. We ask them to trust that we support their learning, and yet we are gatekeepers to their futures. Robertson (2001b) sees this tension as a central paradox in teaching.

When I first read Robertson's (2001b) description of the evaluator paradox, I focused on the dilemma it might cause students as they navigate taking risks with people who will evaluate their work. As I write this chapter, I realize for the first time that Robertson's evaluator paradox can also guide our internal process. Moving into the idea of evaluator paradox, rather than simply coexisting with it, allows us to stay connected with students while we assess their work. To want students to take intellectual risks is to want them to learn and thus meet the standards of the course. When we can hold on to our commitment to their intellectual development and the standards of the course concurrently, we maintain rigor and regard. This stance may even reduce our frustration with subpar student work, as we see dips in performance as teaching opportunities rather than student failures.

Holding on to the dualities of the evaluator paradox positions us to manage the complexity of connected teaching and to be better educators. When students trust themselves and us, they are more likely to take risks and grow (Schwartz & Holloway, 2012, 2014). Furthermore, when we know our students, we are positioned to balance challenge and support (Schwartz, 2009, 2017). To begin to understand assessment as relational practice, we consider the meaning assessment holds in the lives of students and teachers.

## One Student Does Not Seem to Care, While for Another the Grade Is Everything: The Meaning of Assessment in the Lives of Students

While some students are (or act) uninterested in assessment, many are explicitly concerned with grades. They are cognizant of their academic progress— they do not want to repeat courses, and some receive tuition support from employers that depends on decent grades. However, on a deeper level, students may perceive grades, faculty comments, and the tone of those comments as indications of whether they belong in a scholarly community or an intended profession. In this section we explore mattering, shame, and possible selves as constructs that help us understand the meaning assessment experiences hold in the lives of students. We also explore two other factors that may shape student perceptions of assessment: a binary view shaped by early assessment experiences and a generational perspective held by many millennials.

### *Mattering, Shame, and Possible and Provisional Selves*

Concepts such as mattering, shame, and a sense of what is possible may appear to have little relevance in the so-called objective world of assessment. However, I propose that attention to these concepts helps us enrich assessment, even deeply critical assessment, and support students' scholarpractitioner development.

*Mattering.* College is a developmental experience for 18- to 22-year-olds and adult students alike. Eighteen-year-olds enter college hoping to find direction or aspiring to a particular career. Adult students also enter with dreams. From a single mother who wants to finish her bachelor's degree to set an example for her kids to a midlife career changer who seeks more meaningful work, adult students experience shifts in sense of self and of their place in the world. In addition, students of color, students living in (or who grew up in) poverty, immigrants and refugees, and other students with marginalized identities may enter our programs lacking confidence and wondering if we will take them seriously.

Given students' sense of purpose, variations in confidence and vulnerability, and hopes and dreams, their sense of connection with their academic programs and communities is vital (Parks, 2011; Schlossberg, 1989).

> My work on transitions—events or nonevents that alter our lives— convinced me that people in transition often feel marginal and that they do not matter. Whether we are entering first grade or college, getting married, or retiring, we are concerned about our new roles. We wonder will we belong? Will we matter? (Schlossberg, 1989, pp. 6–7)

I propose that interactions with faculty and peers, and assessment experiences, provide vivid cues for students as to whether they matter or belong in school. Mattering motivates us and gives us a fundamental social connection (Jordan, 1994, 2010; Kasworm, 2008; Rosenberg & McCullough, 1981; Schlossberg, 1989; Schwartz, 2013, 2017; Schwartz & Holloway, 2012, 2014). For many students, this sense of mattering and social connection provides confirmation or stimulates doubt as to whether one belongs in school, can make the hoped-for career transition, and can move forward toward one's dreams. Mattering and non-shaming assessment experiences may be powerful antidotes to imposter syndrome.

When I suggest that we aim to provide assessment that does not provoke shame, I am not proposing we avoid giving critical feedback or otherwise simply focus on making students feel good. On the contrary, I suspect that students experience individualized critical feedback as more meaningful than superficial praise. Thoughtful critique that communicates "I think you can do better" is likely more significant than a simple "good job" or even an A without commentary. People know they matter when others are concerned with their well-being and future, not when they simply receive praise (Rosenberg & McCullough, 1981). Students find critical feedback that is specific to their work rather than generalized or rote to be meaningful and motivating.

*Shame.* Mattering conveys worth. Shame, on the other hand, indicates one does not belong (Brown, 2012; Jordan, 1989, 2010). Students may hold vivid or vague memories of public failures in school (attempting to complete a math problem at the board or read in front of other students). In a large-scale grounded theory study including 1,280 interviews, Brown (2012) found that 85% of participants "could recall a school incident from their childhood that was so shaming, it changed how they thought of themselves as learners" (pp. 189–190). Likewise, Vierling-Claasen (2013) suggests that the pervasive notion of math anxiety should be reframed as math shame and that early experiences of math failure (often in front of other students) create deep and lasting shame about one's worth in a social learning context.

Shame reduces motivation, initiative, productivity, creativity, engagement, and tolerance for not knowing and other forms of vulnerability (Brown, 2012; Jordan, 1989, 2010). People steeped in shame may withdraw from the setting that triggers shame (Brown, 2012; Jordan, 1989, 2010). I wonder how often students who drop out of our programs or stall for months at a time in a research process are in fact paralyzed by shame. I do not mean to suggest that whenever students experience shame, there is a faculty member at fault. A teacher's feedback is only one ingredient in a larger mix of experiences and even pre-enrollment traumas that may activate shame. Nonetheless, as connected teachers, we seek to reduce shame in the learning space.

*Possible and provisional selves.* Along with mattering and shame, possible and provisional selves inform the meaning some students ascribe to feedback and grades. "Possible selves represent individuals' ideas of what they might become, what they would like to become, and what they are afraid of becoming, and thus provide a conceptual link between cognition and motivation" (Markus & Nurius, 1986, p. 954). Provisional selves are the self-images people try on when transitioning to a new role or professional identity (Ibarra, 1999). If mattering confirms *belonging*, possible and provisional selves confirm *becoming*.

As with mattering, I suggest that interactions with faculty and peers, and the tone and content of assessment, confirm or refute students' possible and provisional selves. This is not to suggest that we avoid providing critical feedback. We are responsible to students and our programs, institutions, and disciplines to provide assessment that reflects the quality of student work. Particularly in training for professions such as counseling, nursing, and education, we owe it to students who do not meet standards to record, identify, discuss the gap, seek to improve, and then if necessary counsel the student out of the program as early as possible before the student spends significant time and money. Whether working with these students or the majority who do well and graduate, we seek to provide critical feedback with respect and a focus on student potential.

## A Binary and Largely Negative View of Assessment

Many adult students grew up in the age of chalkboards and reading groups and thus had public experiences of success and failure as they were required to complete math problems at the board and read aloud in front of classmates and the teacher. Later generations of students may not have been required to pass or fail in front of the class but have been subjected to extensive standardized testing, once and done indications of success, mediocrity, or failure. As a result, many students view assessment as a binary experience in which failure or even average performance provokes shame—they either did well and felt relieved or they failed (literally or by their own standards) and there was no path for redemption.

Conversely, faculty understand formative and summative assessment. We wish more students would engage with and apply our feedback. We invite students to reach out if they have questions. And yet many do not. Perhaps we need to do more to unravel the binary assessment mind-set. Later in this chapter I will discuss the relational conditions that promote student receptivity and engagement with feedback. For now, I propose we must model our own engagement with assessment. I typically share my writing process with students, including successes and rejections in the journal submission process. I discuss the value of feedback vis-à-vis my growth as a writer and am explicit about my experiences of revise and resubmit. I believe stories are more powerful than my offer to discuss graded papers (though I continue to make the offer when a student fails to grasp a concept or I see other potential growth areas). Sharing our stories may challenge students' view of assessment and help them adopt a developmental framework that will serve them well in future classes and the workplace.

In addition, ideally we can more effectively help students understand various kinds of assessment. Perhaps if our intentions regarding assessment were clear, students would be more likely to see the potential benefit of related interactions and communication. For example, I wonder if most students see our critique and grades as high stakes and summative. By explaining the difference between low- and high-stakes assignments (Elbow, 1997) and formative and summative assessments, while also modeling our engagement in seeking feedback from peers regarding our own work, we attempt to help students see assessment as an opportunity to improve in all stages of their careers.

## A Word About Millennials

Unlike their older classmates who might hesitate to discuss grades, millennials may see grades as negotiable (Espinoza, 2012). While some millennials (e.g., those who identify as Latina/o) might demonstrate respect for authority in accordance with their collectivist culture (Ortiz & Pichardo-Diaz, 2011), others, particularly those who come from individualistic cultures, may bring a different sense of power and authority than preceding generations. For many educators, this millennial mind-set may seem entitled and disrespectful of process and professor. Espinoza (2012) suggests reframing this student approach and recognizing underlying positive characteristics—these students are engaged and want to do well. Millennials seek to understand expectations (they may read the syllabus more closely than previous generations of students) and then anticipate that if they meet stated expectations (including numbers of pages and references), they will earn top grades (Espinoza, 2012). While the student focus on quantifiable expectations may frustrate teachers, we might instead look for preemptive opportunities to describe and discuss additional elements of high-quality work, such as critical thinking and well-supported arguments. This is probably not a one-off discussion but a lesson we need to return to again and again to help students adjust their assessment perspective.

## Frustration, Joy, and Everything in Between: Assessment in the Lives of Faculty

For teachers who imagine assessment as purely objective, a discussion of assessment and the teacher's emotion may seem odd. If you doubt that emotion is part of the assessment experience, ask yourself whether you have ever felt frustrated with student work. Or delighted? I suspect most teachers do not have to think hard to remember student work that was aggravating, as well as work that was impressive. Ideally our emotional response to student work does not guide our assessment, but to deny that we have feelings as we read papers and evaluate projects seems disingenuous. In this section, we explore assessment in the lives of professors as we consider emotion, unseen emotional labor, and power.

Teaching is an emotional endeavor. Faculty in several studies, from across a range of disciplines, identified grading and assessment as sources of positive emotions such as satisfaction and pride (Postareff & Lindblom-Ylanne, 2015; Schwartz & Holloway, 2017) and negative emotions including distress (Lahtinen, 2008), dissatisfaction and disappointment (Postareff & Lindblom-Ylanne, 2015), and frustration (Schwartz & Holloway, 2017; Slater, Veach, & Li, 2013).

### The Unseen Work of Assessment

I suspect that when students imagine us assessing their work, they picture us with a stack of papers or in front of the computer. However, there is a less obvious realm of this work—the unseen labor of assessment. We engage in significant internal processing to manage our emotional responses, subpar or problematic student work, difficult students, pressure from administration, and difficult colleagues (Schwartz & Holloway, 2017). We replay conversations, question our responses, and seek to improve our dexterity in difficult interactions with students, colleagues, and superiors. Moreover, some faculty navigate competing priorities when the administration demands high graduation rates and student work fails to meet departmental and disciplinary standards. In other cases, we resolve complex assessment dilemmas as we consider students who sit on the cusp of pass–fail in a context of varying degrees of effort, alleged personal crisis and obstacles, or perhaps group members who failed to do their work. The following example illustrates a professor's internal process:

*There is this place where you find yourself almost negotiating with yourself. Where is the place? It's not just what your rubrics say or whatever your intended outcomes are, but have you given the student the opportunity to demonstrate what they know, and if they are having difficulty, maybe recalibrate it and redo it and resubmit it. But at some level, you just have to say yes or no and the emotion for me is in the struggle of figuring out whether it's going to be yes or no, and how do I help the students see that. But once that decision gets made, I don't tend to look back on that and worry that I didn't do the right thing. . . . So, I try and be open and allow people a chance to again stub their toe a little bit, but also to improve. If they can't, they can't and you know I don't necessarily love that experience of not giving someone credit, in other words, failing them. But that's part of the learning process as well. But emotionally, it is getting to a yes or no, credit or no credit. Sometimes that's a nuance to very challenging dance, but I'd rather have that dance. —Brian* (Schwartz & Holloway, 2017; quote is from unpublished data from the 2017 study)

Brian's story illustrates the internal negotiation of assigning pass or fail status to student work that is on the cusp. He asks himself if he has done everything he can as a teacher. He considers the possibility of allowing the student to redo and resubmit the assignment. And he acknowledges that failing a student is unpleasant. Other professors in the same study recalled negotiating similar situations regarding student work on the cusp, replaying difficult conversations with students or colleagues, and regulating their emotional investment with students who show declining effort and commitment (Schwartz & Holloway, 2017). The commute home from campus, long walks, and conversations with colleagues are among the spaces that faculty use to engage in and manage this unseen labor of assessment. These negotiations and navigations— deciding about grades on the edge of pass–fail, trying to unwind from difficult conversations with students or colleagues, planning next steps—can be draining and demoralizing. And yet we pay little attention to this aspect of teaching.

Brian's story also reveals connections between assessment and power. An essential element of the teaching relationship, assessment is the primary source of power between teacher and student. Presumably, most faculty do not use assessment to exercise or flaunt their power; nonetheless, the act of assessing student work (and students' awareness that their work will be assessed) is central to the power dynamic.

Reflecting on assessment, faculty are aware of several power-related dynamics (Schwartz & Holloway, 2017). Faculty recognize the power they hold as assessors of student work and student power manifest through faculty course evaluations and grade appeal processes. Power is an inherent aspect of assessment for faculty, and managing this power is an aspect of the unseen labor of teaching.

## Interactions Shape Assessment Experiences

The energy and relational disposition that faculty bring to assessment interactions can significantly shape the student experience of feedback and review. In the following two examples, both shared by people reflecting on earlier assessment experiences, we hear and perhaps, more important, feel the impact of teachers' approaches to sharing their assessments with students. In the first example, a former master's student recalls her professor's reaction after she and her team presented a poster in class. In the second example, Stephen Brookfield discusses interactions with his dissertation adviser.

The first example emerged in a study regarding meaningful interactions between master's students and faculty. While participants were not given a definition of *meaningful interactions*, most chose to discuss positive interactions. However, one participant (an education student) recalled two negative interactions with one of her professors. She remembered the following experience in which the professor was "vicious" in his assessment of her group's poster:

> *I'm about five foot seven and a half. By the time he left, I felt two inches tall. He absolutely decimated our board. . . . He did everything against what this class has been about, what our other classes have been about—constructive criticism, initial feedback, all the baloney, all of the teaching training, all of the positives, all that stuff—did not exist. I was so taken aback by what he had done and how he did it, I couldn't even come up with words to intelligently argue with him. —Ashley* (Schwartz & Holloway, 2014, p. 48)

Ashley recalls her professor's severe dismissal of the group's work and his failure to model and enact the assessment methods he and the program allegedly taught and valued. She felt diminished after the interaction and so paralyzed by his approach that she was unable to engage in the very conversation that may have allowed her to learn from her professor's critique.

In a very different example, Stephen Brookfield reflects on working with his doctoral supervisor. Brookfield recalls their first meeting in which his supervisor declared that the methodology Brookfield proposed did not fit his research question. Unlike Ashley, Brookfield felt motivated by his adviser's critique:

> The interesting thing was that when he put this enormous roadblock in my way I didn't feel resentful or that I was on the receiving end of some kind of power play. To the contrary, I knew he was doing this in my own best interests. The way he gave his direction somehow convinced me he was on my side. (Brookfield, 2017, p. 94)

Brookfield (2017) recalls his supervisor clearly explained why the proposed method did not fit the question and the upsides and downsides to various methodological approaches and helped him uncover and understand his tacit assumptions. This process continued for three years as the supervisor regularly challenged Brookfield's thinking, assumptions, interpretation, and decisions. These conversations often pushed Brookfield to reconsider his work, work that he thought was complete.

> But none of this made me angry. In fact, the contrary was the case. I came to trust him. Coming to trust another person is the most fragile of human projects. It requires knowing someone over a period of time and seeing their honesty modeled in their actions. . . . Teachers who take students seriously and who treat them as adults, show that they can be trusted. (Brookfield, 2017, pp. 94–95)

In Brookfield's reflection, we see assessment as a relational practice. From their first meeting, the supervisor challenged essential aspects of Brookfield's thinking (his very choice of methodology) but did so with an approach that conveyed he was aligned with the student. Notice the physicality of the descriptions: Brookfield feels as if his adviser is on his side, while Ashley feels "two inches tall." Brookfield's supervisor was transparent with his thinking, and this allowed Brookfield to learn through the process and trust that his supervisor's guidance was motivated by his hopes for Brookfield's work, not his own need to manipulate or control. Ashley finds her professor to be inconsistent with the very ideas he is attempting to teach. Moreover, she finds herself unable to engage further with her professor. Conversely, Brookfield indicates the level of challenge might have made him angry, but that in actuality it did not. Likewise, there is no sense of shame as Brookfield recounts the process. Instead, the supervisor's focus and attention conveyed mattering, and his investment in Brookfield's work communicated an investment in what he saw as possible for the young scholar.

A relational approach is intended to create a learning environment in which students trust themselves and us as educators. This increase in trust promotes students' intellectual risk-taking, motivation, and belief in their own potential (Brookfield, 2017; Schwartz & Holloway, 2012, 2014), which then facilitates deeper engagement and learning. Likewise, when we know our students well, we are better able to regulate intellectual and academic challenge; we have a better sense of how to frame our feedback and how to strike the most effective balance of challenge and support (Brookfield, 2017; Schwartz, 2009).

## Increasing Student Receptivity and Motivation

Student disposition, state of mind, and readiness play significant roles in students' engagement in learning. At the same time, we can attempt to encourage receptivity to feedback and motivation via the following strategies.

### Convey That Student Learning Matters

Attention and concern express mattering (Rosenberg & McCullough, 1981). Translated to the higher education context, academic attention and academic concern communicate to students that their learning matters (Schwartz, 2017). Students in two studies, though not asked about assessment per se, described assessment interactions that were meaningful (Schwartz & Holloway, 2012, 2014). According to the students, faculty acknowledged effort, explicitly pushed them to work harder and at higher levels, returned graded work quickly, offered additional time to help students clarify their thinking, and expressed enthusiasm about student work (Schwartz & Holloway, 2012, 2014).

### Provide Specific Critical Feedback

As they developed the concept of mattering, Rosenberg and McCullough (1981) determined people do not have to believe that others think positively of them to experience mattering. Faculty who take the time to provide individualized feedback that is specific to the student's work (rather than generalized and seemingly routine) convey to students that the faculty member is paying attention and cares about the student's learning (Schwartz, 2009; Schwartz & Holloway, 2014). Students notice when comments are cursory or specific. A student who receives thoughtful critical feedback, delivered respectfully and with a tone that conveys a commitment to student learning, may feel that her learning matters more to her professor than a student who receives an A without narrative feedback. In addition, even the student who earns the A benefits from specific responses to help her understand which elements of the paper were particularly strong.

### Acknowledge Student Effort

Students notice and care when faculty acknowledge their effort and thinking (Schlossberg, 1989). Why do students respond when someone notices their effort? Many students need to be intentional about making room in their lives for school (e.g., balancing part- or full-time work with studies, sacrificing time with family and friends, letting go of hobbies and community involvement), and this may make faculty recognition of effort meaningful. More specifically, Schlossberg (1989) suggests adult students are often engaged in caregiving—significant work to care for children and aging parents—that is rarely acknowledged. Likewise, she suggests that adults' effort in the workplace often goes unnoticed. These dynamics may make faculty recognition of student work meaningful. In addition, students who are struggling with imposter syndrome or otherwise lack confidence are likely to benefit from authentic positive feedback regarding effort. Schlossberg identified acknowledging effort as a strategy to convey mattering—recognizing effort communicates that we value students as members of the academic community, and this sense of mattering and belonging is important for student perseverance and success (Parks, 2011; Schlossberg, 1989). We can acknowledge effort, even on work that is otherwise subpar so as to balance challenge and support.

### Communicate Expectations Explicitly

When there is a foundational relationship and the elements of the dynamic relational context are solid, students are likely to hear faculty critique as encouragement and a positive challenge. The following recent graduate recalls feeling directly challenged by his professor, who clearly expected him to work at a high level and succeed:

> But my experience was here's a person who's asking—who's asking a real effort of me. Here's a person who's asking me to really understand something and wrap my mind around it, and so like my—my—all of my urges for like I've got to deliver, like I—he's actually asking something of me, so I like want to pony up, and make it happen, like that's typically how I respond when people's— like when they demand more, I like—I actually want to deliver more. —Eric (Schwartz, 2009, p. 92)

While we may imagine we are always pushing students to do better, I am not sure students remain cognizant of this message. I imagine myself to be a teacher who challenges students, and yet I recall an experience that helped me realize I may not generally convey this clearly enough. Several years ago, I spoke with students toward the end of class, telling them I would be traveling over the coming weekend when they would most likely be finishing their final papers, and I reminded them to review their work thus far so they could ask questions before I left town on Friday. I also said something like "I really look forward to reading these papers; I expect them to be very strong."

The next week, a student commented that she worked harder than usual on her paper because I told the class I had high expectations. I was surprised that what for me was a perfunctory comment provided at least one student with extra motivation. A colleague once told me that when guiding students regarding their final projects, he challenges them to "wow me" and that students often respond with effort and energy beyond what is typical. Those who review drafts or allow students to resubmit papers may also employ this strategy with early version, for example, telling students we look forward to seeing how they develop their ideas in the next draft. We know we want students to aim higher and achieve beyond their own expectations; perhaps we need to say this explicitly.

### Share Our Own Stories About Feedback

As noted earlier in this chapter, we transmit a powerful lesson when we share our stories regarding our own experiences with feedback. Unless they have written for publication, students may assume if we are published, we are naturally gifted writers who submit articles and earn immediate publication. They are unlikely to realize that as professors, we continue engaging in various feedback processes, sometimes experience rejection, and often are required to revise and resubmit to the same or different journals to garner publication. In addition to sharing the ups and downs of seeking publication, I discuss the role of peer reviewers—colleagues and friends who read my work and provide feedback. In telling these stories, I aim to convey that I embrace feedback and constantly seek to develop as a thinker and writer. I hope these stories help students see writing and assessment as iterative rather than binary and as a constant quest for improvement.

### Demonstrate Confident Vulnerability

As we share our stories regarding rejection and feedback, we have the opportunity to not only describe the process but also reveal the vulnerability of submitting one's work for review, feeling the disappointment of rejection, dealing with difficult critique, and then experiencing the joy of success. When we share the emotional aspect of writing and receiving feedback, we model security in the face of critical feedback and resilience in light of disappointment. I believe this makes the process (and us) more accessible to students and can serve to reassure students while also encouraging them to work harder, welcome feedback, take intellectual risks, and, in some cases, imagine more for themselves than they initially thought possible. Sharing our stories not only reduces the power differential but also honors the evaluator paradox as we simultaneously encourage students and hold them to high standards. In making our own struggles explicit, we paint a picture of the life of the scholar-practitioner.

## Relational Assessment in Practice

The energy is almost palpable as Richard J. Murphy Jr. (1993), a professor of English, describes a writing conference with a student named Peter. Murphy begins the story by sharing his first impressions of Peter, who was underperforming in freshman English. Peter had not completed all of his work, and the work he submitted was not strong. Murphy showed compassion, wondering if Peter was struggling with the adjustment to college or was dealing with other problems. Finally, Peter met with Murphy for a writing conference. As they sat together, Peter began to read his paper (a highly personal and revealing essay) aloud, and Murphy was immediately struck by the detail and exceptional quality of the work:

> I cheered as he read, could not contain myself. . . . I laughed and sang with delight at his writing, at his doing it, at his knowing how good it was, at his comments along the way. . . . The thing was that he *knew* what he was doing. It had happened all of a sudden; finally, two-thirds of the way through the semester he had become (perhaps for the first time in his life) a student. School made sense to him there for a moment. He understood. (Murphy, 1993, p. 7)

Murphy clearly conveys that Peter's learning matters when he takes such joy in the student's work. Having viewed Peter as underperforming, he could have entered the conference assuming Peter's work would be subpar. Murphy does not describe his expectations of the meeting, but he was clearly open to being impressed by Peter's work and was comfortable expressing his enthusiasm.

After sharing his delight with the work, Murphy inquires as to how Peter's peers responded to the draft. Peter discloses that he did not share the essay (though he had been expected to in class). Rather than chastising Peter for not following protocol, Murphy shared his perspective. He recalls the conversation:

> "What did the group think of your paper?" I asked Peter.
> "You want to know the truth?" he said. "I didn't read it to them. I didn't want to risk it. I didn't think they'd like it. I didn't think they'd understand."
> I told him I knew what he meant. His whole body jerked in the chair. "You do?"
> "Yes," I said. "I think it's hard to share such things. . . ." Peter took over my sentence. "You don't want to let on that you care about them." And as he finished speaking . . . he settled his big body back into the chair. (Murphy, 1993, p. 7)

In foregoing a correction regarding Peter's reluctance to share the work with his peers, Murphy deepens the learning moment. Instead of clinging to his ideas about process, he offers Peter a raft of acknowledgment. By sharing that he too feels vulnerable when sharing his work, Murphy potentially achieves multiple larger educational goals (we do not know for sure, as the story does not include Peter's reflection on the experience). As Murphy discloses his sense that sharing one's writing can feel like a risk, he demystifies part of the writing process, affirms that one can feel uneasy and still put words to paper, and models confident vulnerability, which is a big step toward future creative risk-taking. Moreover, Murphy enacts Daloz's (1999) description of teacher-mentors: "'Welcome,' they say in a thousand languages, 'to the new world'" (p. 207). By sharing a glimpse of his inner life as a writer, Murphy invites Peter to see himself as a writer, to enter the world of people who write.

Peter initially underperformed in Murphy's class; however, eventually he turned a corner. Likewise, several other students in the examples provided in this chapter were motivated, and interactions were productive. However, we know assessment and other teaching interactions can be far more difficult. In the next chapter, I explore frustration, disruption, and student resistance from a relational perspective.

# 5

# LESSONS GONE AWRY AND FRUSTRATING STUDENT INTERACTIONS

## Dealing With Disruption and Resistance in the Learning Space

Disruption happens. Sometimes our effort is the source of the disruption as our best-intended activities, lectures, or assignments go awry. Other times students are the source as they give voice and behavior to their resistance and defended selves. The focus of this chapter is understanding and dealing with the meaning, emotion, and stress of disruption, rather than the pedagogical, androgogical, or methodological changes one might make in response. I explore these ideas with an eye on improving teaching and sustaining energy and enthusiasm for the work.

The idea of disruption has gained currency, particularly in tech and business discourse where the word often indicates innovation or a shift that causes growth. In this book, we rely on a more conventional definition of *disruption*: "disturbance or problems which interrupt an event, activity, or process" (Disruption, n.d.). Disruption for our purposes includes problematic student work and difficult interactions with students; other complex dynamics (e.g., conflict in student teams); experiences where our constructed learning activities, lectures, or assessments do not work; and other events and encounters that cause distress.

As educators, we routinely engage in improving our teaching. Year after year, we revise syllabi, redesign assignments, shift approaches in the classroom, and seek innovative methods online; we do this not only when we detect a problem but also routinely with the goal of becoming better teachers. While we are accustomed to assessing and revising the strategies and methods of teaching, I suggest we are less inclined and encouraged to understand the stress and potential emotional cost of disruptive experiences. These occurrences can detract from our teaching, deplete our energy, and contribute to burnout; these difficult situations deserve our attention. In this chapter, I propose we can learn to more effectively manage disruption and improve our understanding of and ability to moderate the emotions stirred by difficulty, frustration, and conflict in teaching. This understanding may increase effectiveness, reduce stress, and boost resilience as we traverse the highs and lows of teaching.

## Why Is Disruption Difficult?

On the surface, disruption is difficult for many people because it interrupts workflow and often requires what may be thought of as extra work (Schwartz & Holloway, 2017). For example, I am reading papers and I notice a student has plagiarized. Dealing with this situation will require that I contact the student, discuss the plagiarism (often not an easy conversation), and initiate my school's academic integrity process. The student's plagiarism has added work to my load, and this is frustrating. On a deeper level though, disruption is difficult because of the meanings we ascribe to the disruption and the assumptions we make about people, dynamics, and other elements therein (Schwartz & Holloway, 2017). I explore meaning-making in the following two examples.

### Kyle

In the first case, I reviewed a student paper and realized quickly that Kyle did not grasp the central concept. Several of the examples he provided clearly revealed he did not understand. I was frustrated. This concept was essential in this course. Over time, as I have seen other students occasionally struggle, I have refined how I explain the concept and provided examples of the ways students typically misunderstand it (the very mistake this student has made). So reading Kyle's paper, I was agitated. I wondered, was he not paying attention in class, did he not retain it, does he not care? At this point, I did not entertain that perhaps I was still not explaining the concept clearly, nor did I consider there may have been factors particular to this student's experience making it difficult for him to understand. I just knew I was frustrated. Later in this chapter, I will discuss my next steps.

### Rick

In a counterexample, I recently read a paper wherein another student misunderstood several important concepts essential to a theory. I reviewed the paper, made several comments, and asked the student to call me so we could discuss the areas of confusion. Later that day we talked, and I tried to clarify, also inviting him to call me again if he got confused when revising the paper. That evening, I realized that while students failing to grasp the material sometimes frustrates me, in this case I had virtually no negative reaction but instead viewed the entire engagement as part of the teaching and learning process.

## Analyzing My Responses

A few important factors separated these two experiences. In the first scenario, I had discussed the concept in class several times and even described errors that students often make when they seek examples for their paper. In the second case, Rick was writing the paper for an independent study and engaged with the theory on his own through readings, without the benefit of classroom discussion. This is a big difference and may justify why I had different expectations of these students.

However, as I reflected, I also realized I was making assumptions about effort and commitment. I assumed that given the classroom instruction, any student who still did not understand the concept was not listening, was not trying, or did not care. In the second case, I accepted that a student exploring the concepts for the first time on his own (separate from a lecture or classroom dialogue) might become confused. Moreover, knowing Rick (who often submitted work early and initiated extra conversation about coursework and his professional development) I assumed he had worked hard and for justifiable reasons simply did not understand.

Conversely, I imagined Kyle, who was sometimes a bit flippant in class, might not have worked hard on the paper. While it may be fair to expect a student who has heard a concept described repeatedly in class to grasp it more clearly than a student who is engaging in a solo literature review, I was still making other assumptions that were unfair and may have been inaccurate. I would like to think my emotional responses did not shape my assessment; I knew, in the first case, I needed to be careful about my tone. Kyle may have worked very hard and still failed to understand (and perhaps I did not teach as clearly as I thought!). And, possibly, Rick did not work as hard as I assumed, perhaps he rushed this paper and that was the source of his confusion. In part, my assumptions regarding student effort shaped whether I was frustrated or simply continued teaching. Frustration in the midst of teaching has potential implications for our ability to assess effectively and our well-being.

Timing and structure also influenced my emotional response. The first experience occurred during a busy stage of the semester, and the disruption seemed to take more time. The second happened during an independent study, and I was not in the midst of assessing other student work. I realize this may have affected my mind-set as well. Finally, Kyle's paper was part of a regular assignment, and Rick's was a less formal process allowing for revise and resubmit.      |

While these examples center on assessment, we clearly encounter disruption in other aspects of teaching. For example, our constructions of assignments, learning activities, or lectures fall short or fall apart, and at times students disrupt the learning space. In the next section, we explore disruptions that require us to respond in the moment.

## The Time It All Fell Apart and Other Disruptions Requiring In-the-Moment Response

As I move through this section, I want to be clear I am not urging faculty to disregard their emotions in these sometimes-difficult situations. Rather, I think by naming our emotions, we respect the emotional demands of teaching and can remain firmly in our teaching role. In this section, I share two more situations: one singular incident I believe I handled well, and a recurring scenario that continues to challenge me. I draw on these cases to propose relevant strategies.

### Classroom Chaos

I remember this fondly as one of the bigger classroom fails early in my teaching career. This incident occurred about four weeks into a semester, in an on-campus master's course. I asked students to organize into small groups, and then I explained the activity. A student in one group raised a hand and expressed confusion. I tried to explain the activity and then moved on to another group, whose members also said they did not understand. I asked the students if they were all confused, and most students said yes. I explained the activity again, and they asked questions, and the more we discussed, the more confused the students became. Some of them seemed a little agitated. I realized the entire activity was falling apart, and I could either panic or stay solid and see us through the chaos.

Quickly analyzing the students' questions, I believed I understood why the activity was failing. Given the students' level of confusion and frustration, I invited them to take a 10-minute break and said we would regroup when they returned. I also acknowledged the activity was not working, and I would see us through the moment, saying confidently, "I will figure this out."

I joked, "Someday I'll write about this when I'm trying to get a promotion," and a few students laughed. I felt the tension decrease slightly. The students took a break.

The break not only allowed them to step away from the frustrating activity but also gave me a moment to determine the next steps. When the students returned, I told them I thought I had figured out why the activity was confusing, and either we could try a revised version or if they were too frustrated, I would lecture on the topic instead. A few said they would like to try it again, so I explained it with the adjustment, and the students got to work. Later, as we discussed their small group work, I sensed they learned the central concept. At the end of class, I handed out note cards and invited anonymous feedback, asking them to identify two or three aspects of the concept they learned that night and whether I should use the revised activity in the future, redesign it again, or scrap it all together. I collected the cards, and, tired from the evening, I decided not to read them until the next day. The students unanimously said to continue using the revised activity.

## When Students Dominate the Discussion

I wish I were always that confident and together and able to quickly work my way out of a problem, but I am not. A pervasive challenge I continue to struggle with in the classroom is students who dominate the in-class discussion. Semester after semester I try to get better at handling the behavior of these students, and I know I still fall short. Time after time, when I fail to address it effectively either in class or outside of class, I feel I am failing the other students and failing to manage the learning space effectively. I will continue to unpack this struggle throughout this chapter.

## Strategies

The first step in this process is noticing both the disruption and my immediate response. In the classroom chaos situation, I quickly imagined myself at a fork in the road as I recognized the situation as one that could shake my confidence or one I could navigate calmly (and in the process attempt to model steadiness amid imperfection). Aware that students were confused and frustrated, I felt a responsibility to reestablish equilibrium in the learning space, to return us to a place they could trust. Conversely, when I experience students who dominate the classroom discussion, I do not typically view the moment as a fork in the road; instead I feel uneasy that the student is doing this again (this behavior is often habitual) and unsure of how to handle the moment.

Disruption sometimes rattles us, students, and/or the space in a manner that can negatively affect learning. When the disruption is live and in the moment, we need to quickly discern, "Am I unsettled? Are the students?" Disruption in the learning space is not inherently negative. Powerful learning experiences can cause educative disruption—a student's worldview is challenged, and she pushes against the new framework. Or students confront each other's ideas in the classroom or online, and tension rises. These kinds of disruptions, also known as disorienting dilemmas (Freire, 1970; Mezirow, 1978), can spark learning and be essential in students' biggest transformations. Some degree of discomfort and challenge spurs learning; however, there is a point at which challenge and confusion may become intense frustration or anger such that students shut down.

The following strategies help us deal with live disruption: the balcony and the dance floor, holding the space, transparency, and humor.

## The Balcony and the Dance Floor

"Few ideas are more obvious or more critical than the need to get perspective in the midst of action" (Heifetz & Linksy, 2002, p. 51). The balcony and dance floor metaphor, though developed initially for organizational leaders, transfers beautifully to the teaching context. To be on the dance floor is to be in the midst of the activity or the moment—to feel the push and pull and typically to be an actor in the flow of the action (Heifetz & Linsky, 2002). To be on the balcony is to have a bigger-picture view, to see what is happening and to recognize dynamics. From the balcony, we see the players a little more clearly than when we are in the thick of the action, and we see ourselves more clearly, as well.

> The challenge is to move back and forth between the dance floor and the balcony, making interventions, observing their impact in real time, and then returning to the action. The goal is to come as close as you can to being in both places simultaneously, as if you had one eye looking from the dance floor and one eye looking down from the balcony, watching all the action, including your own. (Heifetz & Linsky, 2002, pp. 53–54)

In the classroom chaos example, I could quickly see the situation from both perspectives. As someone in the midst of that moment, I sensed students were frustrated, and the activity was not working. I was in the middle of the action—or on the dance floor. If I had remained there, I might have gotten frustrated with their frustration or triggered into losing confidence and my equilibrium. However, I moved to a balcony perspective that allowed me to see the experience as one moment in the semester and a teaching career. Rather than feeling caught up in the chaos or allowing the situation to shake my confidence, I prioritized next steps—regain my footing, help the students regain theirs, and then rescue the content and learning (by either revising the activity or lecturing).

If we spend too much time on the dance floor, we are unable to view the situation from a broader perspective, but if we spend too much time on the balcony, we are unlikely to know what is really going on in the action. I find I am developing this capacity to move from the dance floor to the balcony and back again over time. I remember my first few years of teaching, a state I now think of as essentially living on the dance floor—I was so focused on content and my plan, I could not see much else during class. I vividly remember a semester when I realized I could also see the flow of the class in a new way; it reminded me of being able to see the court as a basketball player—being aware not only of what I am doing on the court but also of what everyone else is doing, where we are in the game, and the tempo, flow, and rhythm. Heifetz and Linsky (2002) offered strategies for changing vantage points—imagine yourself in a different role or more tangibly, pull your chair away from the table, even slightly. In addition, I find viewing the disruption as an opportunity to model dealing with difficulty also helps me gain perspective.

## Holding the Space

In the next chapter, I propose our authority as teachers has shifted from vertical (top-down) to horizontal (holding the space). Pre-Internet, faculty authority was fueled in part by controlling access to content. The material students needed to know was conveyed via lecture and texts (typically made accessible by the professor). Today, of course, students can access content (credible or not) online. So our authority as teachers is no longer rooted in having the information but rather rooted in helping students learn how to learn and discern and in creating and managing (or holding) the learning space.

Heifetz and Linsky (2002), from whom we borrow the balcony and dance floor strategy, introduced the idea of holding the environment as a leadership concept:

> When you exercise leadership, you need a holding environment to contain and adjust the heat that is being generated by addressing difficult issues or wide value differences. A holding environment is a space formed by a network of relationships within which people can tackle tough, sometimes divisive questions, without flying apart. (p. 102)

Their work is reminiscent of D.W. Winnicott (1960), who proposed the holding environment as necessary for child development. Winnicott's holding environment begins with parents physically holding their children and continues with other ways in which the safety provided by presence of and connection with parents or other primary caregivers offers a consistent and stable space in which children can develop.

Readers may connect holding the space with the cultural conversation regarding safe spaces. I believe the understanding of safe spaces has been distorted by firebrand pop commentators, elected officials, and others who believe that fragile educators seek to protect the feelings of fragile undergraduates and instead call for everyone to toughen up. This argument reveals a misunderstanding of what goes on in a learning space and the reality that hostile and threatening environments are different from intellectual rigor and disorienting dilemmas. A full challenge of this stance is probably best left to another venue. However, I address it here to say I believe learners need to feel some degree of safety and trust in the learning space in order to learn and thrive.

A learning space needs to be structurally sound and is ideally aligned with intended teaching approaches. For example, when students try to learn in an LMS context that is at best user-unfriendly and at worst unstable, they are thwarted by not only the tangible disruption but also the frustration and eventually negative anticipation that detracts from their ability to be engaged, focused learners. Likewise, a seminar-style class may be less effective in a large classroom with rows of unmovable desks. Faculty often do not have control over the LMS or the classroom assignments and furnishings. However, we are responsible for syllabus, assignment, and learning-activity design. And we have lead responsibility for the culture of the learning space, online or in the classroom. Do we treat students respectfully? Do we bring positive energy to the work? Do we convey care? Do we set high expectations?

To hold the space is to do our very best to maintain a learning environment that is respectful, energized, challenging, and supportive of exploration and missteps that may result from aiming high. Students who sense their teacher is undone because the class is not going as planned may lose faith in the teacher or be concerned or frustrated—all distractions from the learning at hand. So, to return to the classroom chaos example, I recognized I could have begun to doubt myself but instead turned to an additional teaching possibility: the opportunity to model handling a moment gone wrong. I intended to prevent students from further distraction, teach or reinforce a positive professional response, and at the same time maintain my own balance. I strove to stay effective and retain my authority in the room. Retaining my authority was not about needing power but about fulfilling my role and holding the space.

Returning to a situation in which I am not as effective as I would like to be, I reflect on my struggle with dominating students, and I realize perhaps I need to rethink my priorities. I suspect that because I am so relationally oriented, I focus on the student who is dominating the conversation and am so concerned with not wanting to shame or embarrass the student, I lose track of holding a learning space that is good for all students. I can probably balance these priorities somewhat by asking the student to stay after class and discuss the issue, rather than raising it in front of the student's peers. I need to remind myself that only by addressing the situation will I do a better job of honoring the learning space for all students in the room.

### Transparency

Confident transparency may be a Swiss Army knife in teaching, many tools in one small package that looks simple on the outside but is more complex on the inside. Those who seek to reduce the power differential in the teaching relationship tend to value and activate transparency. As we discuss assignments, activities, and assessment, we also share our intentions—the purpose behind our construction of the course.

Transparency also serves as a strategy for dealing with some forms of live disruption, allowing us to reassure students and teach an additional lesson. For example, in the classroom chaos scenario, my choice to be transparent was an essential move. Acknowledging that I realized the activity was not working informed students that I was aware they were confused, did not consider myself infallible, was in the process of trying to fix the activity, and respected their time and energy. I took responsibility for the learning space and acknowledged that plans, activities, and interactions can go imperfectly, and everyone will still be okay. Transparency demonstrated a commitment to students and their learning, my sense of self as lifelong learner, and poise under pressure. This was all possible because I was not emotionally undone, but I knew I would be okay, teach the content, and do my best to regain balance in the learning space.

Conversely, transparency may not be a good strategy when we feel vulnerable. There is a fine line here. Sharing awareness of a lesson gone wrong can be empowering if it helps me feel comfortable in my imperfection. But if I am feeling particularly vulnerable, then sharing that level of unease is not likely to help the situation but may further unsettle students.

Context and players are primary determinants as to whether transparency is appropriate. I would not choose to share that I am struggling with a dominant student with the full class. However, I have had situations where palpable tension arose in class (often stirred by the kind of challenging content Heifetz and Linksy [2002] referred to, content that challenges deeply held mind-sets and values). At times, I have chosen to acknowledge the tension either in the moment or sometimes in the next class, if the tension emerges late in a class session. For example, the following week, I might share with students that I noticed there was tension in the room toward the end of our last class, and I had been thinking about what contributed to that tension and what we could learn from it—and I use this as a starting point for the week's class.

I believe that moving into the vulnerability of imperfection can be a strength-generating move and that grace under pressure is a valuable lesson for students in any discipline. Transparency does not mean disclosing everything that is going on for me emotionally or intellectually but rather sharing enough so I am being appropriately authentic with students in the moment.

## *Humor*

Like transparency, humor in teaching requires confidence and discernment. As noted in chapter 3, humor can increase social bonds, boost morale, and refocus attention (Graham, 2010). Relevant to dealing with disruption in teaching, humor can also relieve tension (Berk, 1996; Garner, 2006; Graham, 2010); laughter can lower our blood pressure, improve circulation, and release endorphins (Berk, 1996; Garner, 2006).

Humor requires clear judgment and sensitivity. "The use of humor can be complicated because it may be highly personal, subjective, and contextual and we cannot always predict the way it will be received" (Garner, 2006, p. 178). Funny to one person may be profoundly offensive to someone else. Faculty should avoid humor that targets students or their identities or is disparaging of specific people or people generally (including specific students and students generally) and even humor that is self-disparaging (Wanzer, Frymier, Wojtaszczyk, & Smith, 2006). Faculty should also avoid all attempts at humor involving sex, vulgarity, substance use, and death (Wanzer et al., 2006).

Instead, students tend to appreciate humor related to course material (if appropriate) and planned shared humor, such as cartoons and movie excerpts (Wanzer et al., 2006). While Wanzer and colleagues (2006) found little evidence of effective unplanned humor, which is the kind suggested in this chapter (humor injected to reduce tension in response to disruption in the learning space), another study revealed that respectful spontaneous humor signals that the humor producer is fully present (Graham, 2010). As discussed throughout this book, faculty presence in the learning space matters to students. Moreover, humor communicates immediacy or a sense of connection. "Humor may be another method for instructors to reduce the psychological distance between themselves and their students, and thereby increase the level of immediacy" (Martin, 2007, p. 353).

I suspect the range for unplanned humor is narrow. Following Wanzer and colleagues' (2006) guidance, unplanned humor in the midst of a disruption in the learning space would clearly not be appropriate if related to students or their efforts or capabilities. Students in Wanzer and colleagues' study generally found self-disparaging humor inappropriate. So perhaps humor regarding the process or inoffensive common reference points is more effective than attempts to ridicule or discredit one's self, even if done with a smile. Perhaps self-disparaging humor hints at a lack of surety or sincerity.

Well-executed humor in the midst of disruption requires and conveys confidence. To attempt humor is to risk failing at being funny, which for some people stirs increased vulnerability. Thus, a teacher who is already unsure in a moment of disruption is wise not to attempt humor so as to avoid deepening one's sense of unease. However, when feeling solid despite a lesson gone wrong, we can communicate our confidence to students via appropriate humor, and this can serve to reassure students that we are secure in our teaching role and able to hold the space.

## Disruption as Student Resistance

Throughout much of this chapter, I have focused on disruption as a site for teaching and learning. I have argued that dealing with disruption often provides an opportunity for us to teach students how to deal with the inevitable obstacles they face in their professional lives. Furthermore, I have suggested that in reflecting on the meanings we ascribe to disruptive interactions, we learn about ourselves and our assumptions. In this section, I turn to disruption as a manifestation of student resistance to learning. We explore forms of resistance, a systemic approach, and Relational-Cultural Theory (RCT)-related concepts.

Tolman, Sechler, and Smart (2017) define *student resistance* as follows:

> Student resistance is an outcome, a motivational state in which students reject learning opportunities due to systemic factors. The presence of resistance signals to the instructor the need to assess the systemic variables that are contributing to this outcome in order to intervene effectively and enhance student learning. (p. 3)

Students may engage in active and intentional disruptive behaviors such as talking in class or arguing with the teacher but are more likely to enact passive forms of resistance such as ignoring (the professor or instructions) or refusing to participate (Seidel & Tanner, 2013; Tolman et al., 2017). "Resistance is a motivational *state* and an outcome of multiple interacting factors" (Tolman et al., 2017, p. 3) rather than an enduring trait or inherent aspect of a student's personality. While faculty may perceive resistance as simply a disruption, we are wise to recognize resistance as a signal and a source of information, telling us something about the student or the learning space (Tolman et al., 2017).

## Forms of Resistance

Resistance is driven by two distinct motivations—asserting autonomy and preserving self (Tolman et al., 2017). Students may assert autonomy in reaction to authority such as university requirements that seem arbitrary or institutional racism, sexism, and other forms of marginalization. Student resistance may manifest as anger, frustration, or resentment.

Likewise, students may resist learning in order to protect the self (Tolman et al., 2017). Students who fear failure may resist engaging as a preemptive strategy. In addition, students who manage multiple competing demands for their time and energy (e.g., family, work, school) may resist engaging in school so as to manage other priorities. Anxiety and fear are typical manifestations of preserving self.

In both cases, whether students resist to assert autonomy or protect self (or a combination thereof), resistance is communicative, pointing to the student experience, student motivations, and the state of the learning space (Tolman et al., 2017). Just as we must work to understand *our* deeper motivations, students are not necessarily aware of the motivation behind their resistance.

## A Systemic View of Resistance

Tolman and colleagues (2017) recommend a systemic understanding of student resistance. They note the tendency to assume students *choose* to resist because they are obstinate or do not care about learning (my initial assumptions regarding Kyle, as described earlier in this chapter). This perspective prevents us from seeing our role in the teaching and learning interaction and fails to acknowledge contextual factors. Only when I could see beyond my assumption that Kyle was not trying or did not care could I revisit my role in teaching the concept that he failed to understand.

A systemic approach that acknowledges student and faculty presence, as well as the dynamic of the interaction and larger contextual forces, provides us with a comprehensive framework, one that can be enacted by moving from the dance floor to the balcony and one that aligns with RCT's attention to power dynamics and cultural context. This systemic view of student resistance laid the groundwork for an important step forward in resistance theorizing, the development of the integrated model of student resistance (IMSR). The IMSR draws on an array of theories and includes six distinct interacting elements: cognitive development, metacognition, environmental forces (including privilege and marginalization, work, and family), institutional culture, classroom occurrences, and the experience of resistance itself (Tolman et al., 2017). The IMSR helps faculty understand and contextualize student resistance and then adjust on various levels, including interactions with specific students, course design, and systemic barriers and marginalization.

### Student Resistance Through an RCT Lens

The work of Tolman and his colleagues (2017) has deepened my understanding of student resistance and is consistent with RCT and a connected teaching approach. RCT provides a powerful lens through which to examine the two forms of student resistance: asserting autonomy and preserving self.

*Asserting autonomy.* Students may resist learning in response to seemingly arbitrary policies and requirements and "professor misbehaviors" (Kearney, Plax, Hays, & Ivey, 1991). A connected teaching approach, based on RCT, calls on us to reduce the hierarchy in the teacher–student relationship. Transparency and a willingness to engage with student questions regarding course structure may help reduce power differentials and thus decrease students' needs to resist authority. Transparency may also clarify our motivations in course design and aspects of our teaching such that students no longer see requirements as random but rather understand the intent behind our decisions. Finally, openness to the message conveyed by student resistance may also point to behaviors we should consider changing such as our own apathy, lateness, sarcasm, favoritism, or other behaviors students consider problematic (Kearney et al., 1991; Seidel & Tanner, 2013).

A connected teaching approach supports student resistance in the face of faculty or institutional racism, sexism, or other forms of discrimination. As noted by Tolman and his colleagues (2017), student resistance in these situations conveys important information and may help us recognize institutional failures or our own blind spots regarding identity.

Bringing an RCT lens to resistance scholarship, I also wonder if some students assert autonomy because they believe the cultural narrative that to succeed is to make it on one's own. Of course, we want students to take initiative, attempt to solve problems, and in many ways drive their own learning; in addition, most will also still need to know how to work collaboratively and within organizational structures. Helping students see that asking for help after wrestling with a problem and being open to learning from others, even authority figures, are not signs of weakness but rather valuable and mature approaches to work and may balance the cultural pressure to believe they can and should achieve alone.

*Preserving self.* Students may resist learning or engagement consciously and may maintain this position throughout their studies. For example, students who are enrolled to secure needed credential but do not value the content of a program may do the minimum required to pass or graduate. These students may not be moveable. However, other students may resist precisely because they want to engage or succeed. Two RCT concepts help us understand this dynamic: relational paradox and strategies of disconnection.

The relational paradox, first conceptualized by Miller and Stiver (1997), suggests when people fear disconnection, they move away from connection or relationship (the very thing they want) to avoid anticipated disappointment or pain. For example, after the first night of class, a group of students spread the word they are going out together. A student, new to the university, is eager to make friends in the cohort, but fearing she will not fit in with the group, she declines to go, thereby foreclosing the opportunity for connection. While the previous example is social, we can imagine this in the teaching and learning context as well. Students who fear that asking a question will bring shame (and thus disconnection) decline to participate in class or seek help. Or a student who imagines their authentic self will be rejected by others in class or by an admired professor may remain quiet or disclose little.

Relatedly, people use strategies of disconnection to protect themselves. When students resist learning in an attempt to preserve self (Tolman et al., 2017), they may be engaging in strategies of disconnection. Fearing failure (and thus shame) a student might stop working or drop classes. Likewise, students may become angry, confrontational, or dominant, attempting to prevent or rupture relationships with faculty or classmates. These moves may seem aggressive and at times arrogant; however, they may in reality signal fear and anxiety. When we sense a student is manifesting resistance emotionally, we are wise to consider potential deeper causes and watch for opportunities to refer the student for counseling.

The following chapters help us continue to understand ourselves as educators and teaching as a relational and emotional practice.

# PART TWO

# INCREASING SELF-AWARENESS
# IN CONNECTED TEACHING

6

# POWER AND POSITION

## Exploring Educator Identity Through an RCT Lens

I suspect that when many of us began teaching, we quickly encountered our position power, or the authority that is inherently part of the role. What is my attendance policy? Will I accept late work? How do I think about grades that are on the cusp? Our position as teachers grants us the authority to make these decisions. In the following pages, however, I wish to address interstitial relational power or how our choices narrow or widen relational space and thus the teaching and learning environment we share with our students. Our awareness and intention regarding power in the teaching relationship significantly shapes the learning space we craft for and with students. While the distinction is artificial, this chapter is organized in three sections: relational power in the teaching role, power as it is shaped and enacted vis-à-vis identity, and a path forward.

### Power Is a Fundamental Energy

Building on Maureen Walker's declaration "power is a fundamental energy of everyday living" (Walker, 2002b, p. 1), I propose that power is a fundamental energy in everyday teaching. Walker's belief stems from Jean Baker Miller's definition: "power is *the capacity to produce a change*" (Miller, 1991, p. 198). With Miller's root definition and Walker's interpretation, we can easily see power as a fundamental energy in teaching; power is our capacity to promote learning. The following example illustrates my assertion.

I write this draft on a Saturday morning at the end of the first week of classes. On Thursday evening, in Social and Cultural Context of Counseling, I attempted to provide examples of identities as social constructs. I confidently described how in "our culture" older adults are not typically held in high esteem, we do not tend to express or act with high regard for our elders, and we often seek to figure out how to care for them but do not hold them as central in the family unit or broader culture.

Later in class, we discussed the experience of first-generation college and graduate students who often straddle two cultures: that in which they grew up and the academic culture in which they study. A student, new to the program so in her very first week of classes (and, again, the first night of this class), pointed out that in many African American families, elders are to be respected, and so even in areas where she felt she knew more than her mother, aunts, and other relatives, she would never voice her opinion or challenge theirs. I quickly realized that the point I made earlier about "our" culture not respecting older adults revealed my limited thinking; I had universalized my own white European-rooted experience (and the messages conveyed in white-dominated mass media and culture) as true for everyone living in the United States.

To admit I had made such an error felt vulnerable (I think this would be true always but perhaps even more on the first night of class). However, I was also aware that one of my deepest hopes for students in this class is that they will recognize, acknowledge, and seek to grow when their assumptions are inaccurate, that they will allow their worldview to expand, rather than hold on to the safety of surety. So the best use of my power in this moment was not to hide my realization and continue but rather to admit my shortcoming, share my limitation, and present it as an essential step in the kind of growth we seek in the course. So I disclosed my thinking with the students. I thanked the student who shared her experience and connected it to my earlier claim about "our culture." I acknowledged that my generalization came from a privileged place that allows me to assume the universality of my own experience.

Later in the evening, as we discussed students' hopes and fears moving forward in the class, a few white students noted that they were afraid that as they move through the course, they might say something offensive to others (presumably students of color). I pointed to my earlier misstep and suggested that engaging with social and cultural context is a lifelong learning process, and ideally we would create a space together in which we felt safe enough to challenge each other, admit when we recognized our limitations, and then learn from the moment and move forward with greater clarity. I suggested that if we could develop trust, we would have a foundation for powerful conversations. And I referred again to my earlier privileged assumption, attempting to make the process feel human, and suggested, "I've already messed up and learned from it, so I hope this opens the door for you all to do the same."

I do not share this to say that I handled it perfectly, but I know that I attempted to respond from a place of authenticity, respect, and transparency. This is my eleventh year of teaching, and I have enough confidence to move toward vulnerability and believe I can be vulnerable and still hold on to the role responsibilities of teaching. The vulnerability in the earlier exchange was revealing that I am still learning, and I still have blind spots in my worldview. I am not suggesting we always go to a vulnerable place in front of the class. However, when I can appropriately reveal my imperfections, I hope I model for students that we can explore the inherent limitations of our worldviews without shame. When we can be imperfect, admit our blind spots, ask difficult questions, and reveal we do not understand, the learning space is expanded.

> The courage to teach is the courage to keep one's heart open in those very moments when the heart is asked to hold more than it is able so that the teacher and students and subject can be woven into the fabric of community that learning, and living, require. (Palmer, 1998, p. 11)

The dominant cultural understanding of power as control brings to mind a dynamic that is rigid, closed, and distant: *I will do this, you will not do that, I will not share anything that reduces my power in this situation, but I expect you to risk not knowing in order to learn.* Conversely, power-with, as suggested by Relational-Cultural Theory (RCT) (Miller & Stiver, 1997), is dynamic. Power-with *is* energy, and this dynamic energy, rather than constraining students (power-over), fosters movement in the forms of learning and development. Power-with serves the essential goals of teaching. "If the goal of relationship is movement and creativity, then embracing power is a necessary function. To disavow power is not an option. The option is to choose how to relate *to* and *through* the power that one has" (Walker, 2002b, p. 3). Perhaps we find power in vulnerability and in listening and responding to the other when we see power not as a zero-sum game but as the opportunity to be authentically with the other so as to expand the learning space.

On the first night of class, described earlier, I could see clearly that sharing awareness of my imperfection and acknowledging I learned from a new student might reinforce one of the most important elements of the class I was trying to convey. At the same time, I could be secure in my teaching role and find strength through deep teaching rather than feigning infallibility. Walker (2002b) offers an approach to guide us in these moments:

Two questions support the process of envisioning an alternative paradigm of power:

1. If power is a fundamental energy of relationship, how does power look when used in service of zest, clarity, mutuality, and affirmation of connection?

2. How might our relationship with power help us to more fully inhabit our lives? (p. 4)

As noted previously, I do not disclose every moment of personal insight with students. There are times when I experience a dip in confidence or some other sort of vulnerability and decline to share this with the class. Nonetheless, some moments of insight or vulnerability may offer us an opportunity to teach a deeper lesson through transparency and power-with. Seeking to lessen the distance between my students and myself by choosing transparency rather than command-and-control has helped me navigate other teaching dilemmas.

Years ago, working in a different department, I was charged with teaching a capstone research seminar. Senior faculty had determined all students would use the same methodology for their capstone project. Though I valued the methodology, I believed it was not the right approach for all students and all questions. However, as a junior member of the department, I decided not to challenge my senior colleagues but rather to teach the seminar as it was designed. In the first seminar meeting, I realized that both students were not only bright but also resistant to the method. They pushed back assertively, questioning why they should have to use a predetermined methodology (I agreed with their dispute).

I felt clear on my position—forcing them to make their research question fit the method seemed disingenuous and as if I were exercising my department's power (though not my own). Both students left the first session without committing to the method. To simply tell them they had no choice felt like an empty power play, on the level of "because I said so," a move that would disregard the students' intellect, life experience, and agency. Anticipating our second meeting, I struggled with this tension.

I decided to balance transparency with respect for my department and colleagues. In our second meeting, I told the students I understood their resistance, and if I had developed the capstone I would have designed it differently. Next, I affirmed that my senior colleagues were thoughtful scholar-practitioners who had taught this course many times and chosen the method deliberately. I told the students I was committed to bringing all that I could to help them design meaningful projects to investigate their research interests while using the department's chosen methodology. I knew they were smart enough to go through the motions and design a simple project to meet the requirement, so I clarified that I valued the experience and their journey as students too much to let them settle just to cross this off the to-do list. Rather I wanted us to work hard together, to find a way to use the method and craft a meaningful capstone inquiry project.

Both students finally signed on, though one remained more reluctant than the other. In the end, they both pursued topics they were passionate about, and their later work and final reporting of the scholarly projects indicated they had moments of insight along the way. My sense is that by using my power as Walker (2002b) suggests—to try to increase energy, clarity, mutuality, and connection—and with the goal of facilitating meaningful movement and learning, we found a way to meet the goals set by the department and engage in meaningful inquiry. Had I not been in my first year in the department, working with senior colleagues, I might have lobbied to change the course. But at that point in my career, I decided to sidestep that battle. Instead I worked with the students, from the stance of an authoritative ally (Brookfield, 2015). Perhaps this is what Daloz (1999) means when he suggests,

> Self-disclosure from the mentor seems to play a crucial part in the full evolution of a mentorship from hierarchy toward symmetry. . . . The student needs to know that he [sic] can trust his teacher. In the early stages of development, authority is enough, but as the student grows, his willingness to trust an authoritative mask without knowing what lies behind it dims. . . . Continued development for the student mandates a decrease in the power of authority. (pp. 170–171)

In the first part of this chapter, I wrote as if all other aspects of the teacher and student relationship are equal, and the only power differential is granted through the teacher's positionality. However, all is not typically equal. RCT reminds us that we cannot understand or authentically navigate relationships without acknowledging the influence of race, gender, nationality, sexual orientation, and other aspects of identity that shape the life experiences and related daily boosts, obstacles, or threats faced by people as they move through the world.

## The Inextricable Relationship Between Power and Identity

If we are to understand power dynamics in teaching, we need to, as much as possible, understand how various identities combine to situate us and students for experiences of privilege and marginalization. We need to know that our identities and how we are met in the world vis-à-vis these identities influence what we expect from and imagine for others and ourselves. Some may resist this call, claiming they do not see race in the classroom or that gender no longer determines opportunity. I ask readers who are resistant to consider the following:

> Imagine how different your life might be if you had been born Black, or White, or poor, or of a different race/class/gender group than the one with which you are most familiar. The institutional treatment you would have received and the symbolic meanings attached to your very existence might differ dramatically from what you now consider to be natural, normal and part of everyday life. You might be the same, but your personal biography might have been quite different. (Collins, 1993, p. 40)

Collins (1993) clarifies that she does not believe "people are doomed to follow the paths laid out for them by race, class and gender" (p. 41), that while these elements frame "opportunity structure" (p. 41), people have choices within their context.

We all live and work in systems (including schools) that privilege and marginalize all who enter (and those who are excluded). If we do not commit to challenge these systems of privilege, we are de facto supporting the system and thus oppression (Collins, 1993). Awareness of privilege and marginalization and choices about conceding, supporting, enacting, or challenging these systems has everything to do with power in the teaching and learning relationship.

Social location sets a context for the lives of teachers and students, including daily manifestations of racism, misogyny, homophobia, transphobia, Islamophobia, and other expressions of hate and violence in our learning spaces and broader culture. I may intend for my classroom to be a hate-free zone, but I cannot lose track of the fact that many students might face hate frequently outside the classroom and this may influence their energy and focus. Likewise, a teacher can see herself as skilled and knowledgeable, but students might make assumptions about her ability based on gender, race, or some other element or intersection of identity.

Muriel Shockley (2013), in her dissertation titled *I'll Choose Which Hill I'm Going to Die On: African American Women Scholar-Activists in the White Academy*, reported the following from a participant:

> I was working with a group of emergent [new] graduate students . . . we were going over papers and talking about my feedback. And one said is your feedback based on your culture? This guy was an English teacher in a

private, white high school, who took affirmative action students . . . and I said no, that's not my opinion, that's APA. Let's go look at page 62 for the guidelines for bias. Would you please turn to pages 170 and 171 on how to cite an index? And would you please turn to this page where it says how you use the words "that" versus "which." (p. 92)

Likewise, Linh Hua (2018), writing about teaching and emotion, shared her experience through a composite narrative:

The next day, I begin class and in the middle of my first sentence, a student raises her hand to ask an off-topic question: what's on the midterm? It is the same student that asked at the beginning of the last class meeting, "What are we doing today?" A student stays after class to say that we are talking too much activism and she wants to learn more about the experience of women of color. She wants to know what it's like to be an immigrant, but she feels that the readings and lectures on women immigrants organizing for better pay is more about politics than about the women's lives. At my office, I receive an email from a student who feels that course content is biased and she feels she cannot relate to the content because it is too antagonistic. She doesn't know anyone who believes that immigrant women should be exploited for their labor. She asks whether these ideas will be on the midterm, because she doesn't agree with them. I get another email from a student who says he is enjoying the class, but he thinks it focuses too much on negative elements and is producing a stereotype of immigrant women as downtrodden. He wants to know if I have read essay X because he thinks it would be useful to me. I respond to tell him that essay X is already on the syllabus, please see week 7. (pp. 77–78)

What strikes me about both of these narratives is not that the students are challenging their teachers but the tone of the challenges as experienced by the faculty. The students are not simply disagreeing; they are interrogating their professors' credibility and baseline knowledge, suggesting the professors' ways of knowing are limited by their identities. In fact, everyone's ways of knowing are shaped by their identities, but the students are implying the professors are unique in this and thereby deficient.

I think it is fair to say that the structure of higher education implies faculty hold legitimate or position power, that is, power that accompanies a particular role (a teacher holds power in relation to students, parents hold power in relation to their children) (Raven, 1992, 2008). However, faculty who hold marginalized identities may not be granted the legitimate power of their positions but rather must display expert power by proving they hold expertise in order to possibly be granted the respect and authority that for majority faculty comes with the job title. All faculty work with some mix of legitimate and expert power; however, minoritized faculty are more often challenged to establish their position through expert power whereas majoritized faculty are granted it by virtue of their position (Hua, 2018; Johnson-Bailey, 2015; Pittman, 2010; Shockley, 2013; Stanley, 2006).

Furthermore, the students in these stories seem to speak from a superior position, not as if they disagree with someone who knows more and holds position power but as people who have the power to critique from above, seeking to correct their teacher's limited view and override the professor's authority.

Brookfield (2017) recognizes that his identity grants him the privilege to admit mistakes:

> As an older white male I can admit to mistakes with little fear of consequences. Indeed, my owning up to errors is usually read as a sign of endearing vulnerability: "how courageous of you to share your foibles and mistakes with us!" Colleagues of color and female colleagues are much more likely to have their missteps interpreted as affirmative action giving jobs to incompetent and unqualified minorities. (p. 27)

### *Our Journeys Are Shaped by Identity*

Our understanding of the student experience is shaped by our own journey. To recognize how our experiences limit our understanding, we need to uncover and clarify how identity has shaped our academic paths. Seeing beyond how our personal sociocultural context has shaped our understanding of the world is a significant challenge for anyone who grew up in a homogeneous environment. My journey to see beyond my own vantage point has been informed by colleagues and friends willing to share their experiences, as well as books and films that provide glimpses into others' life stories.

For example, spending time with the works of bell hooks has helped me see beyond my own experience. hooks (1994) recalls attending a desegregated school: "School was still a political place, since we were always having to counter white racist assumptions that we were genetically inferior, never as capable as white peers, even unable to learn" (p. 4). In reading hooks, I realize I never sensed a teacher, guidance counselor, or other school official thought I was less capable than others because of my race. I did not have to think about race while I was learning. Now as a teacher, I am wise to remember that many students of color in my classes have received messages throughout their lives that they are less capable (and many of these adult students now see their children subjected to the same discriminatory treatment in preK–12). I hear these stories from my students (both about their own experiences and about their children's). I do not change my expectations or hopes for them, but I try to remind myself that I may make assumptions about their motivations, challenges, and even affect that are based on my reality and not theirs.

hooks also helps me see social-class-related conditions I have taken for granted. Coming from a middle-, working-class background I had the essentials necessary for college and graduate school, so I must be mindful that some students do not have the money to buy books, a computer, or Internet at home (or a home). Others may struggle to find child care so they can attend class. More profoundly, reading hooks (2000) I realize plentiful clean water is not universal (reinforced later when the Flint catastrophe is reported nationally). I learn that privacy too is a condition of privilege, as people living in overcrowded apartments share rooms, sleep in hallways, and generally may not have a quiet place to do homework or sleep.

I have artificially separated race and class in this section, and of course they cannot be disconnected. So I must know the history that has inextricably linked race and class, as the United States continues to hold a disproportionate number of people of color in poverty (see *Race: The Power of an Illusion*, California Newsreel, 2003, for the history you may have missed in high school, a history often excluded from curricula). And then I need to learn about white poverty, both to increase my awareness of the challenges these students face and to help me understand why white students who grew up in poverty have a particularly difficult time grasping and believing white privilege (an important element in some of the courses I teach).

Knowing students may be dealing with the effects of marginalization and discrimination allows me to connect with students in their complexity rather than assuming a universal experience or overlooking the nuance of their lives. This is the opposite of saying, "I don't see color" or other aspects of identity. I do not adjust expectations but rather see students as individuals who encounter a unique set of challenges, resources, and experiences. To understand that students live in unique complex realities is to acknowledge that identity power and marginalization are always present in relationships, whether in the foreground or in the background.

## Privilege, Marginalization, and Power in the Learning Space

In the following example, an adviser is blind to the lived experience of a first-generation Latinx community college student who does not yet understand how to navigate the college journey. Instead of realizing the student does not have the received knowledge that students with college-educated parents would bring to the college experience, she shames the student for not knowing. The student clarifies this is their first day on campus, and the adviser reasserts her domination, again insisting the student needs to know something she has said clearly she does not know.

> She's like "So, what class do you want to take?" and I said "I don't know." She said "how old are you?" And I was like "26." She said "What do you mean you don't you know what class you like to take?!" I told her that it was my first day ever in campus, I was lost. All I knew is that I wanted to go to school. She told me "You need something better than that, you need to know what class you want." (Zell, 2010, p. 177)

Advisers hold significant power in the lives of students, probably more so with first-generation students who may be unsure about the workings of higher education, including how to pursue a major and career path. In this example, the adviser's obliviousness to the student's experience, the adviser's lack of interest and compassion, and her demand that the student be someone she was not (someone who knew how to select courses) is a disturbing flex of her position power and identity privilege. We can see the potentially dire implications of this interaction. If the student had any insecurity about belonging in college and her potential to succeed, the adviser's comments and tone likely reinforced these anxieties. Furthermore, the student may leave the meeting resistant to ask the adviser and others on campus for help in the future, fearing additional comments that shame and diminish.

Furthermore, a dismissive "you-should-know-this" reaction by an adviser or faculty member could reinforce and deepen stereotype threat. When people fear that doing poorly on a task will reinforce a stereotype attributed to their identity group, they are less likely to do well on the task (Steele, 2010). The predicament of stereotype threat is not that one necessarily believes the stereotype (studies show this phenomenon influences high-achieving students as well as those who struggle) but rather the added pressure of not wanting one's performance to reinforce society's view of one's identity group and, thus, the self.

The insidious impact of stereotype threat extends beyond the act of test taking or task completion. In related studies, researchers discovered that Asian students, who expected to do well in calculus, were more likely to study in groups, whereas Black students were far more likely to study alone. While collectivist culture likely plays a role in Asian students' tendency to study in groups, researchers also found that Black students' frustration with calculus, their concerns about whether they belonged in college, and their fear of reinforcing relevant stereotypes drove them to try to push through calculus on their own (Steele, 2010).

When we shame students for not knowing (course content or how to navigate college), we potentially drive them further into isolation, which may lead to continued poor performance or failure. Conversely, by meeting students where they are and welcoming them into a learning conversation rather than shaming them for what they do not yet know, we can help students reframe asking for help as a manifestation of strength and a routine strategy rather than a source of shame. What better use of our power as teachers?

Imagine how the conversation between the student and her adviser described earlier in this section might have unfolded differently. If the adviser had recognized that the student lacked information about course selection, she could have asked supportive questions to ascertain the gaps in the student's knowledge. Did the student know which courses were available? Did the student understand the system of courses, including the meaning of course numbers and prerequisites? Was the student unclear because she did not understand these procedural elements, or was she unsure of major and career goals? Had the adviser approached this discussion willing to meet the student where she was, the adviser might have seen the opportunity to help the student learn to navigate the system, build related confidence, and either discuss choice of major and career goal or at least make an appointment at the career center for a related conversation. This meeting could have been the gateway, a moment of welcome and development for this student, but instead she was put down, shut down, and dismissed. The adviser missed the opportunity to have a life-changing conversation.

Likewise, when students are situated in privileged identities and a professor holds marginalized identities, the authority necessary for successful teaching can be disrupted. Indira Nair, professor emerita of engineering and public policy at Carnegie Mellon, recalls early in her career that students sometimes seemed to view her simply as "a foreign woman" and doubted her knowledge (Nair, 2018). In response, she routinely included complex problems in her lessons that would require her to make intricate calculations quickly in front of the class; this typically established her credibility with students.

If she had not thought to display her computational prowess at the start of the semester or were otherwise less secure and thus threatened by the students' sense of superiority, she might have spent the semester struggling with student resistance, dismissiveness, and even harassment. Moreover, research has shown that students tend to evaluate women faculty more harshly, while assigning more positive attributes to male faculty (Boring, Ottoboni, & Stark, 2016; MacNell, Driscoll, & Hunt, 2014). So privilege and marginalization in the learning space have implications beyond a given semester, potentially influencing faculty evaluation and promotion.

Faculty with marginalized identities may face a difficult balancing act of both proving their competence (despite degrees, title, tenure, and other markers that would typically indicate credibility in the academy) and not seeming "too powerful." One colleague told the story of a department chair who asked her to change a student's grade and reported that students found her to be "too formidable" and "intimidating." Privilege and marginalization shape power in the learning space.

## Identity and Power: A Way Forward

Four strategies help us move forward with greater intentionality: understand self, understand others, bring less-heard or unheard voices to the conversation, and challenge systems that marginalize and oppress.

### Understand Self

Only by understanding self can we recognize how identity shapes the power available to us and our students. In the ways any of us are privileged, we can begin to understand our power and identity if we are willing to confront our privilege directly and own up to the ease and access it provides (Collins, 1993). And in our own experiences of marginalization, we may benefit from working to undo assumptions and narratives that have served as survival strategies but may also block our ability to connect with others (Collins, 1993).

### Understand Others

To be a committed teacher is to care about students' lives. I am most able to meet students where they are if I have some sense of their life experience.

> Empathy begins with taking an interest in the facts of other people's lives, both as individuals and groups. If you care about me, you should want to know not only the details of my personal biography but a sense of how race, class and gender as categories of analysis created the institutional and symbolic backdrop for my personal biography. (Collins, 1993, p. 43)

Those of us who teach in the social sciences, humanities, or fine arts may be more likely to gain a sense of our students' biographies as we read their papers, review their creative work, and hear their stories in class. Those who teach in other disciplines may learn more about students' lives through advising, attending student organization events, and engaging with a range of voices on regional, national, and international levels via programs, books, articles, blogs, and films. When we have a broader awareness, we can more effectively use our power to create an inclusive learning space.

## *Bring Less-Heard or Unheard Voices to the Conversation*

If you do not already include readings or other materials by scholars of marginalized identities and practitioners in your discipline, find them and inject those voices into your course. Too often our courses reveal the work done only by privileged and mainstream voices who have had access to publishers, research funding, and other support. Too often, students of color see themselves reflected only in assigned readings in courses on race, queer students only in queer studies, and women only in women's studies. When all readings for a course are written by white heterosexual men, the course reinforces the cultural narrative of supremacy and may keep emerging minoritized scholar-practitioners at the margins. Students may need to see thought-leaders who share their identity to imagine themselves with a seat at the table.

## *Challenge Systems That Marginalize and Oppress*

Do something! If you notice transgender students are being marginalized by faculty, contact your faculty development coordinator and suggest a training session on understanding and supporting transgender students. Investigate whether university policies are trans-inclusive, and if not, lobby your dean or provost. Likewise, when you notice other forms of systemic oppression in your institution, take action. If you feel stronger in collaboration, engage colleagues to work with you (ideally colleagues who also hold privilege; do not automatically turn to minoritized faculty to confront the systems that oppress them). Trying to solve the entirety of oppression in our institutions is a daunting task that often paralyzes well-meaning folks of privilege into doing nothing. While we are not expected to finish the work of undoing oppressive systems, we have a responsibility to do our part (Hertz, 1945, *Pirke Avot,* 2:21) and to leave our communities better than we found them. Do something and then do something else!

## Power as Energy to Expand the Learning Space

As noted at the beginning of this chapter, the distinction between position power and identity power (or marginalization) is artificial. Identity and position interact for faculty and students, often increasing or diminishing power in the teaching relationship. In addition to the clear interplay between position, identity, and power, a further connection emerges as the final theme in this chapter. Returning to the wisdom shared by Maureen Walker (2002b), power is the energy of everyday teaching. When we opt for power-over or command-and-control, we constrict the learning space. Conversely, through various expressions of power-with, such as measured and confident vulnerability, transparency, appropriate shared decision-making, and committed and ongoing attention to identity (ours and our students') and the larger cultural context, we expand the shared learning space. Again, recalling Walker (2002b), we seek to use power "in service of zest, clarity, mutuality, and affirmation of connection" (p. 4). Finally, a nuanced understanding of and relationship with our position, identity, and relational power helps us to more fully inhabit our roles as educators and manifest our deepest hopes for our students and ourselves.

In the next chapter, we explore teaching and emotion.

*7*

# EMOTION AND TEACHING

## Recognizing Transference and Moving Toward Relational Clarity

*I was frustrated and I couldn't quite get insight into what was going on with this student. I felt like she was meeting with me too often, being too dependent, wanting me to determine her thesis question, and then she would go away and not really seem any more directed. I got more and more resistant and annoyed, it seemed like she wanted it to be my idea not hers.*

*It triggered all the rescue fantasies that teachers have—every time she called, I returned her call immediately. I kept going back and forth between wanting to rescue her and make it right and being annoyed.*

*When I began to think about strategies, I realized that my feelings of being overwhelmed, annoyed, and conflicted were part of a pattern I had experienced with my daughter who was not taking responsibility for herself in some ways. I realized I was so annoyed because it hit close to home. Once I understood that annoyance/rescue contradiction and developed some strategies, I was less annoyed.* (Amanda, September 2017)

I would like to say that I see the best in each student and the learning opportunity in each interaction. But, occasionally, like in the previous example, I find myself frustrated or reacting to a student. Sometimes students or moments seem to touch a nerve in a manner that appears disproportional to what is really happening. Other times, I catch myself making assumptions about an individual student or group of students before I even get to know them. I have found over time that when I recognize these very human reactions and assumptions early, I am able to adjust my response, which makes me a more effective teacher and tends to reduce my stress. When I fail to identify these dynamics, I am more likely to react to a student in a manner that does not reflect their actions or work, and this makes me less effective and more likely to remain frustrated, angry, or otherwise stressed than I would if I could see the dynamic from a broader perspective.

In this chapter, I draw on the Relational-Cultural Theory (RCT) concept of relational images to explore these dynamics and be proactive and intentionally responsive. Some readers will recognize the connection to transference and countertransference, as described in the psychoanalytic literature and later applied in the teaching milieu. These concepts add to our discussion, and I provide a brief overview in the next section. Following an introduction to transference and countertransference, I define *relational images* and consider how they may similarly shape our interactions and relationships with students. Later in this chapter, I continue to draw on literature pertaining to transference, countertransference, and relational images and expectations to identify strategies for recognizing and managing these dynamics.

In the following pages, I focus primarily on these concepts as they relate to our work with particular students in the dyadic context. However, some faculty will experience similar dynamics with classes or cohorts wherein a group takes on a particular vibe or energy because of the mix of personalities or a few dominant students. The concepts and strategies provided in this chapter can be applied to understanding our feelings about groups of students as well.

## Transference and Countertransference

Educators seeking to understand the intensified emotions we sometimes experience in response to students have tended to draw on psychoanalytic literature, in particular the concepts of transference and countertransference (Robertson, 1999b; Schwartz & Holloway, 2017; Slater, Veach, & Li, 2013). Some readers of the current book may either resist or be deeply familiar with a psychoanalytic framework and may wish to skip ahead to the section on relational images and expectations. However, for others, I provide a brief review of the psychoanalytic perspective. Robertson (1999b) described transference as

> an unconscious displacement of thoughts, feelings, and behaviors from a previous significant relationship onto a current relationship—a phenomenon that teachers and students both enact with each other, sometimes resulting in a dramatic intensification of those relationships. (p. 151)

Transference was introduced by Freud, who initially suggested that patients unknowingly project ideas about people from their past onto their therapist, noting that these ideas could be accompanied by either positive or negative feelings (Robertson, 1999b). Freud later identified counter-transference, acknowledging that therapists might react to clients' transference. Subsequent critiques of Freud disputed his claim that therapists would have such a response only to a patient's transference and not experience transference based on their own unresolved and deeper constructions and impulses (Hayes, 2004; Robertson, 1999b).

For many contemporary scholars and practitioners, acknowledging that therapists and teachers can experience their own unprovoked transference reduces the power differential and is more realistic than earlier models that saw therapists and teachers as infallible. Throughout the rest of this chapter, I will typically use the term *transference* to describe this phenomenon as understood from a psychoanalytic perspective. Like Robertson, I choose to use the term *transference* rather than *countertransference* to acknowledge that faculty may experience intense emotions stirred by their own inner frameworks and unrelated to a student's possible transference. However, when drawing on the work of those who prefer the term *countertransference* to describe the experience of the practitioner (e.g., Hayes, 2004), I use *countertransference* to respect their conceptual positioning.

Finally, although we might be more likely to recognize transference evidenced by unpleasant feelings toward a student such as anger or frustration, transference can also engender positive feelings. Heightened positive emotions such as disproportionate enthusiasm, joy, or felt need for connection with a particular student signal transference as well. These feelings can lead faculty to interact with students inconsistently, favoring some while overlooking others or otherwise seeming to value some students and their learning more than others.

## Relational Images and Expectations

As we learn to navigate our world early in life, our experiences shape our sense of what we can expect from relationships. These expectations, about both relationships in general and specific kinds of relationships, are relational images (Jordan, 2010; Miller & Stiver, 1995, 1997). For example, we might develop a general sense that when we try to engage with other people, they respond positively, or that people are generally closed off to connection and so when we reach out, we risk rejection. Or, more specifically, through our earliest school experiences, we might grow to believe teachers are friendly and can be trusted or they are mean and expect us to misbehave and fail.

These images are either reified or challenged over the life span, and they guide us as we enter new relationships. For example, a young person who experiences his pre-high-school teachers as interested in his progress and confident in his potential is likely to assume that high school teachers will hold him in the same regard. A new graduate student, who as an undergraduate connected with at least a few of her professors, might be more likely to approach and engage with her graduate faculty than a student who did not have such experiences (Karpouza & Emvalotis, 2018). Conversely, a student who felt shame when asking faculty for help may assume future contact with professors will also result in similar feelings and may be less likely to engage.

Students arrive in our classrooms and online learning spaces with relational images of teachers—assumptions about what it might be like to engage with us as faculty. A student who is confused by a reading and assumes that if he asks the professor for help, he will be perceived as incapable and dependent may avoid seeking help without realizing he is making an assumption based on past experiences. These relational images typically work on an unconscious level, so we may not see where our assumptions are preventing us from engaging in meaningful interactions or relationships.

Attempting to counter negative relational images when I teach courses that include several first-semester graduate students, I discuss relational images explicitly. My hope is to challenge students who think faculty are not approachable or that we do not want to hear from students when they are struggling. I aim to help students see interaction on the graduate level as possibly different from their previous experiences and thus to be more likely to seek help or contact regarding research ideas, future goals, and related aspects of professional development.

As they developed this idea, Miller and Stiver (1997) used the term *relational images*. I suggest that the term does not do their concept justice. From my perspective, *images* is rather static. While it might indicate that we develop mental models of relationships (e.g., teachers are like this or when I ask for help I am likely to get a certain response), a deeper reading of Miller and Stiver's work reveals a more complex phenomenon. I propose that the concept of a relational image, as intended by the founders, is in actuality a multifaceted *anticipatory relational construction*.

Miller and Stiver intended us to see relational images as more than pictures of people and relationships. They suggested that relational images are our *expectations* of potential interaction with others, how those interactions will feel, and the *meaning we make* regarding relationships and interactions (Jordan, 2010; Miller & Stiver, 1997). For example, if a student imagines that her professor is eager to be helpful and that approaching a professor is a reasonable step, she (the student) is likely to expect she will be met with positive regard and find the interaction useful. So she imagines that the interaction will be positive; this may sound so obvious as to be trite, but I suggest that for many students, imagining that an interaction will feel either positive or negative (enriching or dismissive) plays a significant role in their decisions about when to get help and from whom and when to engage in other ways (e.g., volunteer for a research project, approach a professor about the possibility of graduate school). As she anticipates the interaction, our fictitious student also likely makes meaning, for example, that she is worthy of connection and belongs in the academic community. If, however, she has generally experienced negative interactions with teachers, she might assume that she is not worthy of others' support and does not belong in school. I suspect this meaning-making is often under the radar. While a negative interaction may literally cause us to question whether we belong, perhaps more likely these moments of separation quietly contribute to feelings of doubt and disconnection from learning communities.

Just as students arrive with relational images and expectations of faculty, we too have formed our own expectations regarding students (Robertson, 1999b; Schwartz & Holloway, 2017; Slater et al., 2013). These frameworks and assumptions emerge from several sources, including our experiences as students and with our own teachers, our early and later teaching experiences, and our relationships with other significant people in our lives (including our parents, siblings, spouses, and children). The following examples help us explore relational images.

*Vince.* Vince reveals the thing that upsets him the most when working with students is when they say he is not available or that they have trouble reaching him. He acknowledges that students who do not work to their capacity frustrate him but that over time he has learned the adult students he teaches may have competing priorities or other reasons why they are not as devoted to school as he wishes they were. He says he has learned not to take it personally when students do not engage deeply. However, he realizes that suggestions he is inaccessible or unresponsive upset him more than any other interaction with students. Vince says he is available to students and considers himself to be more responsive on e-mail than many of his colleagues. In some cases, he says he receives this feedback from students who in fact *dropped out of contact with him*, making the student claim even more questionable. I asked Vince if he had a sense of why these accusations were so deeply troubling.

> *I guess you could probably go back to some childhood issues maybe. I always seem to be in the wrong place at the wrong time. I remember working for my father years ago and he had a bar . . . and any time I would run out to get lunch my father would show up and it always seemed like—it has always been*

*a sensitive thing to me. It is almost like if I am working down here in my office but happen to run in to watch maybe some of the hockey game . . . you know, my wife will come down and say "I thought you were working." I always seem to get caught in that moment. —Vince* (Schwartz & Holloway, 2017, p. 49)

*Lad.* An associate professor of English, Lad Tobin thoughtfully explores teaching and emotion in *Writing Relationships: What Really Happens in the Composition Class* (Tobin, 1993). In a section titled "Reading Myself Reading My Students: A Classroom Example," Lad recalls,

> I was especially bothered by the four eighteen-year-old male students who sat next to each other, leaning back in their desks against the wall. They usually wore sunglasses and sneakers with untied laces; they always wore baseball caps . . . they joked or smirked . . . rolling their eyes or talking to each other. . . . At first I tried to ignore them, not to let them get to me . . . [but] I was always aware of them, even when they weren't acting out. . . . What was going on? I was usually relaxed and comfortable with students. I was reasonable. I was well-liked. So, the problem had to be with them. They were threatened by me, I told myself, so insecure that they had to stick together and act tough. (pp. 33–35)

Lad explains that he assumed these students were distracting other students in the class, but he did not confront them because he did not want to reveal that they were annoying him. When the four students met with him individually for writing conferences, he was surprised when they were polite and at least moderately engaged. He continued to see them as "insecure adolescent boys" (p. 34) and tried to ignore them, but they continued to act out in class. At one point he lost his temper with them and in an angry voice told them not to sit together anymore. Eventually he realized that these students evoked strong memories of his experience in high school, times when he behaved similarly and times when he felt competitive with other male students: "I realized how much, for whatever reasons, I was still bothered by the group behavior of adolescent males" (p. 35).

Both Vince and Lad revealed relational images and expectations in their stories. When students tell Vince they cannot reach him, he experiences the feedback as if it is coming from his father or wife, two people with whom he is intimately connected. His experiences of his father and wife are that they routinely assume he is not working and seem to find him only when he is taking a break. Clearly, he does not have the same length or depth of history with his students, and yet he realizes that their comments evoke the same shame and anger. He acknowledges that he has even had this frustrated reaction in situations where he was actively trying to engage with a student who has been unresponsive. In these cases, Vince might see clearly that the student is unavailable, not him; however, he becomes angry, and this seems to confirm his relational expectations (that others do not see how hard he works) and overpower what might otherwise be a clearer assessment of the student feedback and situation.

Lad's story also powerfully reveals the influence of relational images. He vividly describes the four students, including their posture, sneakers, ball caps, and sunglasses. He acknowledges he was distracted by them even when they were not disruptive and that he expected them to be rude and disengaged when he met with them individually. He realized that he came to teaching with images and expectations of adolescent males and that his assumptions were based on his high school experience, his own acting out, and memories of feeling competitive with his peers.

Lad realized early that he was in constant mental conflict with the students and attributed the conflict to them, assuming they were insecure and rebelling against his authority (Tobin, 1993). His assessment may not have been incorrect—the students may have lacked confidence in the college classroom and have developmentally still been working out their relationships with authority figures. Regardless, Lad's effectiveness with these students was affected by the degree to which he was reacting to them, which was disproportionate to what was really happening in the classroom. His work with these students was impacted, and we can imagine that the tension affected his presence in the classroom overall. Moreover, he reveals that at one point he fantasized about getting revenge by failing them all, and while he quickly caught himself, he also recalls he was surprised when they were polite and at least moderately attentive in conference (Tobin, 1993). Lad's projection of what to expect from adolescent males shaped his perceptions, and then his experience reinforced his preexisting relational images and expectations.

Having finally unpacked why he was so triggered by these young men, he began to engage with them more intentionally. For example, he made room for their struggles with authority by inviting them to critique the assignments and his assessments; three of the four students responded well and began to produce better work (Tobin, 1993). Lad's story powerfully illustrates the central point of this chapter (and this book): We should not deny that we experience these emotions, nor should we imagine we will reach a state where we do not have them. Rather, by understanding our emotions more deeply, in this case learning to more quickly identify when we are having a disproportional reaction, we can increase our effectiveness as teachers and spend less time in heightened negative emotional states.

## *Why Do We Develop Relational Images and Expectations?*

Just as we make split-second assessments to move through our days safely (e.g., Is this stove hot? Is the traffic far enough away that I can cross the street?), we also quickly assess the possibility of connection with others. We are neurologically hardwired to connect (Banks, 2015), and our survival depends on being in relationship with others, so assessing whether it is safe to reach out is serious business.

I think that at the very least, most students sense their academic careers will be smoother and more successful if their teachers believe in them and if they can develop relationships. This belief is both strategic (if I can ask questions and get help from my teachers, I am more likely to succeed) and existential (if I connect with my teachers, I belong in this learning community; if I do not belong, maybe I am not worthy as a student or even as a person).

In addition, I suspect that most people who teach also want to feel some level of meaningful engagement with learners. Thus, connecting with students, being held in positive regard, and sensing that students think we are good at what we do are typically desirable conditions of the teaching life.

We do not teach simply to connect or receive compliments or to be liked, but I suggest we are happier and thus more effective and resilient when we feel connected with our students or at least that they respect us. Vince and Lad both reveal the deep disturbance that accompanies a sense of being disrespected or thought of as uncommitted or unavailable. I suspect that an absence of praise is not necessarily a problem in that we assess our worth as teachers based on a variety of reference points (e.g., are students engaged, are they generating quality work, can I see progress over the course of the semester). However, dismissive student behaviors and communications can be painful, because, as noted earlier, when we are pushed away by others, when we feel disconnected, we tend to craft a story about why the relationship is not working, and we ascribe meaning to the situation (Miller & Stiver, 1995).

For example, Lad initially blamed the students and decided they were insecure and immature—a perspective that likely shaped how he approached his interactions with them. Other teachers in a similar situation might have assumed that the fault was theirs and they were not capable of connecting (e.g., a new faculty member might fear she is incompetent, whereas an older professor may assume he is losing his relevance). To try to avoid this pain of disconnection and related stories we tell ourselves, we activate relational images and expectations to help us navigate safely and try to avoid the disconnection before it happens.

We can imagine that Lad's quick assessment that groups of adolescent males are going to be difficult was a protective strategy so that he could, in theory, shield himself from feeling diminished by them as he did with his high school classmates. However, while a hot stove is always hot, certain kinds of students who remind us of others in our past are of course not literally the people who have shamed or marginalized us previously but rather may be quite open to engaging positively. And even when they are not ready to engage, as in Lad's case where the students were acting out, we are more effective if we can remain centered in our best teaching selves (as he eventually did when he provided productive options for them to channel their feelings about authority) rather than when we react disproportionately based on past experiences.

Context also powerfully shapes relational images and the experiences that reignite the feelings attached to those images. As noted throughout this book, RCT reminds us that we are inextricable from our sociocultural context (Jordan, 2010; Miller & Stiver, 1997; Walker & Rosen, 2004). A gay or lesbian student who has a lifetime of being shamed regarding identity may expect the same treatment from professors. Female students who have been repeatedly marginalized by male faculty may enter classrooms with trepidation as to whether they will be taken seriously. Students of color who have been disregarded by white teachers in the past may assume white faculty will not see their potential. Similarly, faculty who have been marginalized based on aspects of identity may be cautious with each new class of students.

These examples are understood more deeply when we draw on the pivotal work by Patricia Hill Collins (1999). Collins describes these kinds of marginalizing ideas as *controlling images*—constructs created by those in power to justify the oppression of others. Collins (1999) begins by interrogating the pervasive images of Black women in U.S. culture and then extends the reach of her work: "These controlling images are designed to make racism, sexism, poverty, and other forms of social injustice appear to be natural, normal, and inevitable parts of everyday life" (p. 70).

Social institutions such as schools, media, and the government repeat and reify these images to rationalize oppression and retain dominant group power. For example, if systems and individual educators convey the idea (the controlling image) that Black students do not work hard or care about school, they can avoid even considering the existence of systemic racism that may be interfering with these students' abilities to succeed. Likewise, if the message (controlling image) is women cannot do well in technical fields, there is no reason to explore the possibility of sexism in related academic departments. By placing the blame on identity groups' alleged inherent deficiencies, those in power justify inequality as the natural order and retain their control through systems and the cultural discourse.

Controlling images not only fuel dominant groups but also present obstacles for those who are marginalized, who must undo and see beyond these controlling images that, again, are presented as natural and inevitable (Collins, 1999). A young Black woman who wants to be an engineer may be fighting a lifetime of negative messages about her potential, messages that might be deeply ingrained in her sense of self, as well as frequent reminders in her academic relationships that she does not belong and will not succeed. We can see how controlling images shape relational expectations.

In addition to cultural context, students are exploring shifts in identity that accompany engagement with school (Kasworm, 2008), and some adult students may be in the midst of personal or professional crises or transitions that leave them questioning their worth (e.g., divorce, failed attempts at promotion, or extended unemployment) (Miller & Stiver, 1995, 1997).

Likewise, as faculty, we bring our own vulnerabilities—novice teachers wonder if they can succeed, veteran teachers wonder if they are still relevant, and many faculty feel insecure about managing technology in the classroom and in online spaces. As asynchronous online courses increase in number and popularity and as elected officials and others continue to question tenure, teaching practices, and even the essential value of higher education, faculty may also feel their worth is being assaulted in the broader culture. All of these vulnerabilities make us susceptible to fears of disconnection, marginalization (a form of disconnection), and perhaps even feeling obsolete; as our fears are heightened, we may become more likely to be triggered by relational images and expectations and the related meanings we attach.

## Application: A Framework and a Process

Fortunately, over time we can reshape relational images or, at the very least, learn to recognize when we activate them and adjust our responses accordingly (Banks, 2015; Jordan, 2010; Miller & Stiver, 1995, 1997; Walker, 2004). A return to the literature regarding transference and countertransference in concert with RCT provides strategies for recognizing, understanding, and responding to these assumptions and emotion-laden experiences.

### An Organizing Framework

Hayes (2004) provides a foundation for application, a framework in which he proposed that countertransference can be more clearly understood by considering "its basic constituents, namely the origins, triggers, manifestations, effects, and management" (p. 28).

*Origins* are the unresolved conflicts (Hayes, 2004) or relational images (Jordan, 2010; Miller & Stiver, 1995, 1997; Walker, 2004) that are at the core of these intense reactions we sometimes have with students. Lad's high school experience with adolescent males was the origin for his experience with the four young men in his class. Vince's exchanges with his father were the beginning of his feeling that his hard work remained unseen.

*Triggers* are the events (Hayes, 2004) that awaken the original conflict or relational images and expectations and spark an emotional response. For example, the moments when the students in Lad's class acted out were triggering events. Similarly, he acknowledged feeling fixated on them even when they were not acting out (relational images), and he expected them to be disrespectful and disengaged in conference (relational expectations); these phenomena serve as triggers. Similarly, Vince was triggered when students claimed he was unavailable or unresponsive.

"*Manifestations* are the affective, behavioral, cognitive, and visceral reactions" (Hayes, 2004, p. 29) that faculty experience when triggered. Lad reported feeling distracted, unsettled, and angry, and he fantasized about failing the students; these manifestations generate *effects* (Hayes, 2004) on the professor's teaching practice. We can imagine that Lad's effectiveness in the classroom was affected by the level of distraction and emotional distress. We can also wonder to what degree the four students sensed his hostility, which then fed their insecurity and need to protect themselves by acting out. Similarly, Vince expressed anger and frustration, remembering students who claimed he was inaccessible, and we can wonder how this affected his work.

Lad's story ends with powerful examples of his *management* of the situation. He recognizes his emotional state, uncovers the origins and triggers, and then recenters himself in his teaching role, for example, encouraging the students to critique him, which serves to sharpen their critical thinking and provide a productive venue for their struggles with authority. Grounded in his professional role, he is a more effective teacher and has also reduced his distress, as he is no longer triggered by the students.

## *Identifying and Understanding*

Hayes (2004) suggests that practitioners seeking to identify and understand transference or relational images will most likely notice manifestations first and be able to identify triggers and eventually origins second. This process describes Lad's experience wherein he noticed his disproportional anger with the students, then realized what had triggered his response (the students' behavior), and finally traced back to the origin (memories of his high school experience). Likewise, Vince initially recalled his frustration with students when they charged him with being unavailable. He later realized his experience was shaped by interactions with his father and his wife.

Broadly speaking, heightened emotion (particularly that which seems disproportionate to the situation) or an urge to act or treat a student atypically signal that we are being driven by transference or relational images (Hayes, 2004; Jordan, 2010; Miller & Stiver, 1995, 1997; Robertson, 1999b; Schwartz & Holloway, 2017; Slater et al., 2013; Walker, 1999, 2004). Specific examples of feelings and tendencies that may indicate transference include the following:

*Intense Feelings in Response to a Student*
- Feeling intensely angry, frustrated, or even joyous in response to a student
- Experiencing an intense response if a student misses an appointment or class
- Feeling personally attacked by student criticism or feedback
- Noticing that when you interact with the student, you feel as if you are interacting with someone else in your life (e.g., child, parent, spouse, coworker)
- Feeling more relaxed with one particular student than with others
- Fearing a student though there is no clear reason for the sense of alarm
- Feeling profoundly disregarded by a student ("I spent so much time with you . . . and you just gave nothing back" [Slater et al., 2013, p. 10])
- Experiencing an overidentification with the student
- Feeling jealous or competitive with the student
- Believing you know the student more deeply than is realistic
- Feeling sexual or other intense attraction to a student

*Urge to Treat a Student Differently Than You Treat Other Students*
- Feeling tempted to give the student a break or help that is not consistent with how you treat other students
- Feeling compelled to rescue a student
- Intensely questioning your judgment regarding a particular student
- Engaging in disproportional self-criticism regarding work with a particular student
- Feeling tempted to embarrass, shame, or fail a student

Upon noticing any of these signs, we are wise to attempt to identify the trigger. Possible triggers include student behaviors such as skipping meetings, working below their potential, dropping out of contact, cheating or plagiarizing, or responding to faculty with disrespect or a confrontational attitude (Hayes, 2004; Robertson, 1999b; Schwartz & Holloway, 2017; Slater et al., 2013). Triggers that emerge for faculty internally include feeling as if a student reminds us of someone with whom we had a complicated or damaging relationship (Hayes, 2004; Jordan, 2010; Miller & Stiver, 1995, 1997) or deep struggles with our insecurities as teachers. When the manifestations are clear but the triggers are not obvious, we might ask ourselves whether there was a particular moment in the interaction with the student in which we felt our emotions escalate and whether the student reminds us of someone else.

This is also a time to return to ideas regarding relational clarity: Are the emotions that I am experiencing connected with my own experience, or am I taking on the student's experience? For example, I feel frustrated with a student who is doing subpar work and has missed a few classes. I believe the student is smart enough to get an A but is not working hard. If I acknowledge my frustration and move on from it, my response is proportional. However, if I find myself furious with the student or deeply disappointed, I may be, on some level, experiencing the student's choices and work as if they were my own, blaming myself inappropriately, or feeling invested in a student's success beyond what is realistic.

After identifying manifestations and triggers, we are then positioned to consider origins. This deeper reflection will help us reconnect with our professional role and responsibilities and will (along with an increasing awareness of manifestations and triggers) help us preemptively identify possible transference or influence of relational images and expectations in the future. Building on the earlier example, when I realize I am having a disproportional reaction to a student who is not doing well academically, I review whether I have done all that is appropriate for a teacher to do in these cases. Could I legitimately offer more support or guidance? Have I checked with the student to see if there is a crisis or something else interfering with school? If I have done all that is appropriate, I can regain clarity that the student is making choices about how hard to work, and those choices are separate from my teaching.

When I gain relational clarity, my frustration with the student does not disappear but is decreased, and this helps reduce my stress. I see the situation more clearly and respond to the reality, which is that the student is choosing not to work hard or has a constraint that is prohibiting hard work. In addition, in the future, when I sense a similar frustration with a student who is not doing well, I run through my checklist of appropriate responses and then release the tight grip on my perception of the student's effort. To be clear, many of us as dedicated teachers strive to help students who are on the cusp of failing or otherwise quitting school. When we can do this without profound emotional pull and arousal, this is probably a balanced manifestation of our commitment as educators. However, when we feel heightened anger, frustration, or despair regarding a student, we are likely operating on transference or relational images. And from that intense state we are less effective as teachers and more stressed overall.

## Managing Transference and the Influence of Relational Images in the Moment

Upon identifying transference, relational images, and possibly their triggers and origins, we are positioned to manage our approach. Jordan (2010) provided a shorthand we can use to check ourselves: Are we reacting or responding? When we *react*, we are likely being driven primarily by our own images and expectations; when we *respond*, we are present with students and simultaneously clear on our role and responsibility. For example, if I feel angry with a student who consistently arrives late for class, my experience may be fueled by frustration with some other person in my life. However, if I note that the student is late and feel disappointed but not agitated, I can then respond by, for example, asking her if there is anything she would like to share about why she is late. I might learn that she is often required to work late, has unreliable child care, or is late for no good reason. This discussion about reacting and responding may stimulate questions regarding authenticity. Is reacting somehow more authentic and responding less so? Walker (2004) suggests that exploring our emotions amidst and in reflection regarding the intensity of relationships is to be authentically professional, whereas to simply react is to possibly cause disconnection and thus less ably fulfill our professional commitment.

A first step is to quickly assess whether we are firmly grounded in our teaching role and if not to consciously return to that role (Jordan & Schwartz, 2018; Robertson, 1999b; Slater et al., 2013). Lad exemplifies this when, responding to his insight, he identifies teaching strategies to deal with the students' resistance. When this move seems difficult, we might rely on the balcony and dance floor strategy described in chapter 5 (Heifetz & Linksy, 2002). On the dance floor, we are intensely in the moment; however, moving to the balcony, we may be able to access a broader perspective that goes beyond immediate emotion and also regain connection with the responsibilities and goals of our role as teachers. In addition, Robertson (1999b) reminds us to avoid discussing our transference with students (unless we teach in a discipline such as psychology or social work where it may be relevant in a supervision context).

A second step is to draw on our personal strengths such as empathy and insight (Hayes, 2004), compassion, and facilitation skills. I remember feeling unnerved by a student who challenged my authority in the classroom, and by reminding myself that despite feeling unsettled, I am a good facilitator, I was able to regain my footing and continue teaching from steadier ground. By reconnecting with a strength, I moved away from feeling unsettled.

## A Proactive Approach to Transference and the Influence of Relational Images

Along with strategies for dealing with these dynamics in the moment, we are wise to proactively position ourselves to more quickly identify and respond to transference and the influence of relational images. The foundation for this work is to "cultivate a receptive attitude" (Robertson, 1999b, p. 161). Transference and related dynamics are part of the human experience of teaching and occur across disciplines and regardless of class size, learning setting, undergraduate or graduate context, and instructors' years of experience (Robertson, 1999b; Schwartz & Holloway, 2017; Slater et al., 2013). If we accept that we are human beings engaged in a dynamic human process (teaching), then it follows that we bring our histories, relational experiences, and imperfections to our work. Thus, to be open to the notions of transference and relational images is not to admit weakness but to invite insight and manifest strength.

When we approach intense emotional moments in teaching with curiosity rather than resistance, we can then reflect on our experience and seek to gain clarity (Hayes, 2004; Robertson, 1999b; Slater et al., 2013). Using the questions identified earlier such as *what particular moments set me off* and *does this student remind me of someone else in my life* (Hayes, 2004), we can further unpack our experiences. Although these prompts might help us manage a situation, a return to these questions later, outside of the intensity of the moment, provides additional awareness. This kind of reflection might also help us identify patterns or what we perceive to be student types that trigger our emotions (Robertson, 1999b). Lad realized that groups of young males were a trigger; Vince recognized that accusations that he was not available piqued his anger. By identifying our patterns and triggers, we can often catch ourselves much earlier in the process (e.g., "I know why I feel anxious—this kind of interaction unnerves me") and regain our footing more quickly by returning to our educator role, thereby teaching more effectively and reducing stress.

In addition, identifying discrepant relational images can help us challenge our relational expectations. Discrepant relational images are the images that counter dominant cultural narratives and our own embedded relational assumptions (Jordan, 2010). In the earlier example, Lad would do well to remind himself of adolescent male students who were attentive, engaged, and respectful. Vince could recall experiences wherein his effort was recognized by students and colleagues. Jordan (August 2017) suggests that when we find ourselves reacting to students, we look for an image that counters the dominant discourse or our inner dialogue.

Finally, Robertson (1999b) and Slater and colleagues (2013) remind us to seek out and engage with trusted colleagues or other professionals for confidential support. Robertson (1999b) argued that teaching—as a complex human and relational endeavor—holds many parallels to other helping professions (e.g., counseling and social work) wherein professionals are expected to engage in supervision that is confidential and allows practitioners to be vulnerable and imperfect without facing professional consequences. While the concept of supervision will likely not appeal to many who have chosen a faculty path in part for its autonomy, faculty developers, deans, and department heads might consider offering professional development sessions to introduce and give credence to these concepts within faculty communities, not only to educate new and seasoned faculty but also to create a climate wherein faculty can discuss these experiences and dynamics without shame or fear of judgment. Likewise, academic leaders might provide relevant training to faculty mentors who can then open the door for novice teachers to begin exploring these intense emotional experiences, helping them to understand "as I teach, I project the condition of my soul onto my students, my subject, and our way of being together" (Palmer, 1998, p. 2).

In the next chapter, I continue exploring significant teaching challenges: deep disappointment and failure.

# 8

# DISAPPOINTMENT
# AND FAILURE

## When Teaching Almost Breaks Your Heart

I write this book with feisty optimism and a deep belief in the power of connected teaching. I recall students and classes who touched my heart. Energy flowed, and learning was deep. Students sometimes struggled but then overcame, growing into the learners or scholars they would become. I learned too, refining my approach and becoming a better teacher. The students seemed grateful, and I was as well.

Conversely, at times connected teaching has nearly broken my heart. These experiences have been rare, but this book would not be complete if I did not address the despair of having it all fall apart. I am thinking of times when I felt I created meaningful learning experiences, brought my best self to the classroom, and tried repeatedly to adjust when our work together ran amiss. Despite it all—student mood, lack of energy, and obstinance sent a clear message—many students were not learning, resented the class, and were frustrated with me. To respect the confidentiality of the students involved, I will not describe my own experiences but rather turn to examples published by other faculty. I am grateful to these colleagues for sharing their difficulties and in so doing, helping us consider our own.

Professor Richard J. Murphy recalls such a semester when he taught graduate teaching fellows, supervising their teaching of first-year English:

> A number of them had grown very dissatisfied with the program and my direction of it. Every meeting with them seemed to me to be charged with the potential of increased frustration or ill will. The course I conducted for them in the teaching of writing was unsatisfying to us both. . . . Though normally I kept my door open, by the end of that year it was closed. The

experience of working with these students paralyzed me. I don't doubt that I was responsible for my share of that year's failure. I believe now that my sense of their alienation stiffened me, made me less adaptive or resilient, led me to say things that only alienated them further. No attempt at resolving our differences seemed to work. (Murphy, 1993, pp. 99–100)

Murphy's honesty provides a window into processing and moving on from these most difficult teaching experiences. He owns his disappointment and interrogates his role in the downward spiral. He is not blaming himself exclusively but rather sees both students' imperfections and his own. As I read his words, I imagine self-acceptance balanced with a wish to do better and a hope for brighter semesters—this helps me begin reflecting on my own fraught experiences. In the following sections, I explore the impasse and downward spiral, the psychological contract, and misperceptions between students and teachers. I also offer strategies for dealing with profound disappointment in teaching and relevant preemptive approaches.

## The Impasse and the Downward Spiral

Central to these experiences: we think we are doing our best and yet students resist both us and learning; students perceive the course as unfair and, concurrently, we think they are unduly resisting the work; and though we try and try again to fix the course and reconnect with students, the problems feel insurmountable.

These particular experiences reach an impasse—a point at which we feel we are teaching with integrity and our expectations are reasonable, and yet students rebel—submitting late and/or subpar work, voicing complaint in the classroom or withdrawing into silent protest, or more formally reporting their upset to a department head or dean. Such a situation seems untenable and unfixable; neither conventional teaching strategies nor connected teaching approaches help. Instead our attempts at repair fall short—whether we alter assignments, offer additional support, or attempt to discuss the problems, the chasm only widens and a downward spiral ensues. Students simply want to be done with the class and so do we. But we cannot walk away and neither can students—we all have to finish the semester. We persevere, trying to repair and yet the disintegration and pain continue.

No faculty are immune to such an experience, which can hit new and seasoned teachers alike. Sociology professor Cheryl Albers recalls volunteering to teach an upper-level honors seminar, believing that designing and teaching the course would allow her to pilot new approaches and teach some of the best students on campus:

The unexpected initial reactions of a number of students constituted one of the most disappointing professional experiences of my long career. . . . I spent months excitedly designing a course that I believed would be both challenging and engaging for the most select students on campus. . . . To my bewilderment, a third of the class expressed dissatisfaction with the grounding of the class in student directed learning. They wanted a more teacher directed experience—clearly not the reaction I anticipated while I was enthusiastically designing the course . . . by the midpoint of the semester, about a quarter of the students were still resisting the basic structure of the class. (Albers, 2009, pp. 270–271)

Albers's description reveals surprise and disappointment—she enthusiastically designed a course she thought would engage students and instead they resisted. She recalled feeling defensive about her approach and that the semester caused her "dismay."

While the timetable of teaching—the changeover in semesters, students' enrollment and graduation—is often a plus given that each new semester and cohort provide the opportunity to try again, the transitory nature of work with students may also contribute to the deep disappointment of these experiences. One instructor, who had also worked as a college administrator, recalled,

*I think that one of the reasons my classroom failure has hit me so hard is that you don't have much opportunity to recover. As a dean, when I knew I had lost my way with the staff or pissed someone off about a decision I made, there were countless ways to recover. The relationships were different, more permanent, not always authentic, but often deeper. But in the classroom, I feel like you get one shot because students are transient, at times less reasonable, with a consumer mentality.* (Janet, June 21, 2018)

This inability to repair the breach may lead to feelings of loss. For those trying to teach from a relational perspective, these impasses and spirals challenge our core beliefs about teaching, our capacity, and the passions that first draw us to the field.

Teaching experiences that go so wrong can rock us to the core, bruising our sense of efficacy, identity, and purpose. Teaching is a complex and intense endeavor—to do it well, one has to be all in, and for many of us this means that being a dedicated passionate teacher is central to our identity. When we reach an impasse, similar to Murphy's (1993), in which "no attempt at resolving our differences seemed to work," we may feel as if there is no logical next step. This is not simply a lesson gone wrong, but our entire approach and our deepest beliefs are called into question. We feel as if we have lost a part of ourselves, and, indeed, we have. So how do we move forward?

## Is This Failure?

Searching for frameworks to inform these most difficult teaching experiences, I sought literature regarding workplace failure. Some resist the language of failure, seeing it as a binary and perhaps self-defeating construct, too easily internalized as "I failed" or even worse "I am a failure." I respect these critiques. To be clear, I am not suggesting that teachers or students *are* failures, but rather that there is worth in using failure as a construct to consider these experiences. Failure is "the inability to meet performance standards or expectations" (Newton, Khanna, & Thompson, 2008, p. 228). In addition, *failure* is "a complex phenomenon. Its occurrence reflects convergence between an individual's particular constellation of strengths and limitations and a unique set of circumstances. . . . It involves personally acknowledging the inability to achieve desired results and managing public criticism" (Newton et al., 2008, p. 241). I find this definition particularly powerful, as it suggests an interaction of strengths, limitations, and a particular set of circumstances—all combining for an "inability to achieve desired results." Failures of the sort discussed in this chapter are certainly public, at least within the class and possibly beyond.

Relevant to teaching and my earlier points about a sense of loss, Newton and colleagues (2008) described "a psychologically meaningful failure experience" (p. 229) as one in which achievement is central to one's identity and self-worth; one feels personally responsible for the outcome; a lack of success is consequential to one's psychological, professional, and/or interpersonal domains; and one's definitions of *success* and *failure* are tied to the process. Newton and colleagues clarified that all people experience failure during the course of a career and that those who have had significant professional failures experience stages associated with grief: denial, anger, bargaining, depression, and acceptance—again, echoing the sense of loss described earlier in this chapter.

One does not have to look hard to identify teaching experiences that fit the definition of *psychologically meaningful failure*. Teaching in disciplines we love, working with students for whom we hold expectations, we channel our intellect and creativity into the work. When we encounter students who seem uninterested, unable, or actively resistant, we may feel at least disappointed and at most as if we have failed. "One of the biggest killers of morale is the sense that our efforts are in vain. To labor diligently to no apparent effect destroys the soul" (Brookfield, 2017, p. 85). As noted previously, a sense of failure can also reinforce or unsettle our sense of self as educators. Failure can reify imposter syndrome for those who fear that at their core, they are unqualified to teach. Both new and seasoned teachers wrestle with impostership (Brookfield, 2017) and worry their self-perceived incompetence will be discovered by others.

> The further we travel from our habitual practices, the more we run the
> risk of appearing incompetent. . . . In the midst of experimentation it's
> not uncommon to resolve never again to put ourselves through the experi-
> ence of looking foolish in front of students. . . . The moments of failure
> that inevitably accompany change and experimentation increase the sense
> of impostership by emphasizing how little we can predict and control the
> consequences of our actions. (Brookfield, 2017, p. 229)

Ironically, the very confidence and willingness to critically reflect that pushes us to take risks and improve our craft may lead to failure, which then elicits a return to feelings of ineptitude and impostership.

## The Psychological Contract Between Teachers and Students

Constructed to explore assumptions and conflict between employees and organizations, the psychological contract is relevant to the teacher–student relationship and helpful in understanding our perceptions of impasse and downward spiral experiences as described in this chapter. Psychological contracts are unwritten assumptive agreements based on tacit understandings of perceived workplace norms and reciprocity between employees and the organization (Rousseau, 1989, 1990). They can be classified as transactional (e.g., expecting compensation for agreeing to chair a program) or relational (e.g., assuming that if we work hard and with integrity, we will be treated with respect and regard) (Frey, 2018; Rousseau, 1990) and, I suggest, sometimes a combination thereof. Educators have begun using the psychological contract to understand academic work. For example, Bordia, Hobman, Restubog, and Bordia (2010) applied the psychological contract to understand students' psychological well-being and satisfaction in collaboration with their thesis adviser. And Frey (2018) applied the psychological contract to explore workplace and organizational betrayals as experienced by higher education faculty, such as when administration cancels a degree program without discussion or notice.

A multifaceted psychological contract tacitly shapes the journey students and teachers take together. Students assume and expect we will provide a well-designed learning experience including readings and other content, teaching or instruction in some form (e.g., lecture, facilitation, supervision), purposeful assignments, and fair assessment. They expect us to arrive on time, return assignments promptly, and teach ethically. Students also expect courses to be organized and stable. I am repeatedly struck by how unnerved students seem when I make what I believe are minor adjustments to the syllabus (even in response to something like a class cancellation due to bad weather). Likewise, faculty assume (or at least hope) students will attend class regularly and on time, complete assignments, and otherwise engage in learning with integrity and ideally some degree of interest and energy. Perhaps this sounds obvious and even naive—anyone who has taught knows, for example, that occasionally assignments we create do not work well, and some students are enrolled simply to secure a needed credential and do minimal work. However, applying the psychological contract to further understand tacit assumptions (ours and our students') and the emotional toll when these assumptions are not met helps us further understand the frustrating and demoralizing experiences that are the focus of this chapter.

For example, the readings we assign and students' responses to those readings may seem straightforward—we select materials, and then students choose whether to engage. If they do, they may or may not find the materials meaningful. However, the degree of student frustration when readings appear inappropriately difficult or irrelevant and our disappointment when students do not seem to read are noteworthy reactions. Likewise, graded assignments may seem transactional and yet are loaded with possible conflict, as students and teachers may disagree about the clarity and import of the assignment, quality of work, and veracity of assessment.

Returning to Murphy's story, we see evidence of the psychological contract and related violations:

> The course I conducted for them in the teaching of writing was unsatisfying to us both. Some of them regarded the journal and paper I asked them to write and the books I asked them to read as unduly burdensome. I regarded their unwillingness to enter into the spirit of the work as refractory and in some cases irresponsible. My praise of individuals' writing or teaching was discounted as untrustworthy, and my criticism was resented as unfair. (Murphy, 1993, p. 100)

As quoted earlier in this chapter, when Murphy (1993) describes the semester, he recalls no longer keeping his door open, feeling paralyzed and less adaptive and resilient in response to the alienation he perceived in his students. His story evidences the toll of psychological contract violations, which are more than benign unmet expectations. Rather, these violations can potentially evoke feelings including anger, resentment, harm, a sense of injustice, and rupture to the relationship (Rousseau, 1989).

Somewhere in the teaching exchange between Murphy and his students, one side or the other felt let down by their counterpart. Perhaps students first found the course material troublesome and then responded by decreasing their engagement, which in turn caused Murphy to withdraw. Or maybe Murphy was less engaged than was typical, or the course was not as well designed as he thought, which caused students to pull back from him and the work. Either way, both students and teacher felt the other was not living up to their side of the implied bargain. When these baseline expectations were unmet, students and teacher alike became resistant and withdrawn, transactionally and relationally. Each side was more than mildly disappointed in the other and seemed to have a deep emotional response, believing their counterpart did not manifest basic responsibilities in the endeavor.

Murphy's story also reveals how this kind of rupture can spiral into further hurt, withdrawal, and counterproductive behavior. There is a lot on the line in teaching and learning—students want to do well and progress, and teachers want to feel as if they have effectively facilitated learning. So when the spiral begins, both sides may not only be disappointed or angry at the other's perceived failure but also fear their own shortcomings. This fear may motivate decisions to avoid or do minimal work and to withdraw as much as possible to avoid further hurt and sense of failure. The combination of disappointment and pain and resulting behaviors further erodes trust, which is essential in relational teaching.

## The Failure of Perception

Students and teachers navigate the learning space on at least three levels: explicit expectations, implicit assumptions, and deeper psychological makeup (Holloway, May 29, 2018). The syllabus conveys our explicit expectations regarding assignments, due dates, assessment, and other aspects of the course. Per the psychological contract, students and teachers also bring implicit assumptions to the learning space—expectations regarding everything from punctuality to respect. And we all bring the power and marginality of social cultural identity (seen and unseen), a host of other life responsibilities and challenges, and our unique psychological makeup. So as we and our students meet in the learning space, elements of these layers shape our sense of self and other—our momentary, reflexive, and reflective perceptions are based on assumptions that may be faulty.

Teachers and students alike may misperceive who and what is involved in shaping the other's actions and responses. For example, we may feel that a class is a disaster, that there is a wave of discontent. And yet the negative energy may stem from one or two vocal students. Jennifer Snyder-Duch, professor of communication, asks,

> I wonder how often this cycle is initiated by one student. How often does this one student's resistance or frustration disrupt the class (either in front of the professor in the classroom or in outside conversations with class-mates), cause the professor to withdraw or tire, which then causes several more students in the class to feel negatively toward the professor or class. (Snyder-Duch, June 29, 2018)

Likewise, I suspect students often imagine we are entirely in charge of the course or research project, when in fact we operate in a larger context that might shape our approach. For example, students may be unaware we are locked into using a department-mandated syllabus or required assessment rubric or have been pressured to teach a course outside of our specialty. Students may blame us for something they see as faulty in the course that is not of our design. In some cases, we can be appropriately transparent and help students understand the structural elements at play; however, other times such disclosure may feel inappropriate or seem self-serving.

In addition, we and our students often remain appropriately unaware of profound challenges outside the learning space that affect the selves we bring to the work. Personal and family health, relationship disruptions and transitions, financial stressors, job pressures, job loss, and mental health challenges such as depression and anxiety can alone or in combination alter our ability to bring our best selves to students and their ability to bring their best selves to their studies. I firmly believe there are limits to what students and teachers should share with each other, and yet these outside elements can have an impact.

I recall a semester during which I needed to schedule surgery and allow for recovery time. I developed a plan with the dean to complete in-class work with students two weeks early, take time off for the surgery, and then read students' final papers (submitted as originally planned by the last week of the semester) from home. I thought this plan would provide minimal disruption, and because I am a rather private person, I initially declined to share the reason for the change. Soon after I announced the plan, I realized I felt awkward about making such a significant shift without explanation. So I told students I was having surgery.

A few months after the semester ended, a student told me that initially, students were upset by my changes to the schedule. They speculated reasons for the change, none of which justified the disruption, further contributing to their frustration. She noted that after I disclosed my pending surgery, they understood and were far less frustrated. Sometimes we and our students rightfully choose not to share the details of our lives. I share this story not to encourage uncomfortable or inappropriate levels of disclosure but rather to illustrate the degree to which a lack of information and ensuing assumptions can disrupt the teacher–student relationship.

In the previous example, students made assumptions about faculty behavior. Flipping the equation, Albers (2009) recalled an experience in which her assumptions about students proved understandably wrong. She imagined honors students would be more open to innovative teaching approaches than other students. However, her shift away from teacher-directed learning unsettled these students, who were accustomed to a conventional classroom hierarchy and were possibly more successful than some of their peers because they were so adept at navigating the traditional learning structure. Moreover, Albers (2009) realized,

> While I assumed Honors students would be the most receptive to my disruption of norms, I found that their status made them especially invested in maintaining the status quo. . . . The scholarship funds they receive are dependent on maintaining high grades. (p. 278)

Albers's example is powerful in part because these were motivated and high-achieving students—these students were not resisting the course structure simply to avoid working hard. Yet, the very aspect of these students' identity that she perceived as a right fit for an innovative approach led them to dissent throughout the semester.

Holloway (May 29, 2018), a counseling psychologist, suggests when students find themselves unsettled by some aspect of the implicit contract or deeper psychological tension, they may not see the root of their upset and so attach it to an easier-to-identify element of the explicit contract. Her insight corresponds to workplace literature. Organizational studies research (Jensen, Opland, & Ryan, 2010) suggests employees faced with breaches in the psychological contract may respond with counterproductive work behaviors such as abuse (e.g., ignoring others or making disparaging comments), intentional failure, sabotage, withdrawal, or theft (which perhaps translates to academic dishonesty in the teaching and learning context)—though identified in the workplace, these behavioral responses are also evident in our classrooms and online.

So, for example, students who find complex readings overwhelming may not consciously know they feel betrayed by a professor who they believe is expecting more than they feel capable of; instead they complain about the amount of reading assigned each week (which positions the professor as unreasonable instead of exposing the students' real struggle with the work) or simply decline to read. I am suggesting not that feeling overwhelmed is a legitimate reason to stop reading but rather that although student resistance may manifest as frustration with the explicit course structure it may really be about a deeper struggle.

## Moving Forward

In this section, I draw on a model for dealing with failure and additional material regarding the psychological contract to help us find a way forward after these deeply difficult experiences.

### *Navigating Failure*

I understand why some may resist the language of failure. Whether one finds the word *failure* to be useful or problematic, the following model offers a concise process for finding our way out of these seemingly intractable situations. Newton and colleagues (2008) proposed a three-step model for successfully navigating workplace failure: "recognizing that failure has occurred, restoring and/or maintaining emotional equilibrium, and learning the appropriate lessons so that one can move forward as a more effective worker" (p. 227). They provided a shorthand for the model: Stop. Regroup. Learn.

*Stop.* Stopping to recognize the situation as failure is an important first step. When we recognize failure in the midst of the experience, we might be able to make productive adjustments. Whether we recognize failure in the midst or after, naming the situation is powerful psychologically, as it "signifies an ending point, closer to a death than a misstep, allowing people to begin to come to terms with the experience and move forward" (Newton et al., 2008, p. 233).

> Actually acknowledging failure can bring a sense of relief. It closes the door on an often emotionally claustrophobic situation. It signifies directly facing the fears that have kept one stuck. But acknowledging failure also brings its own psychological challenges—dealing with assaults to self-concept and self-esteem and the accompanying negative emotions triggered by the experience. (Newton et al., 2008, pp. 235–236)

Seeing the failure situation as concluded allows us to begin to reflect, process, and consult with others so as to gain clarity.

*Regroup.* Next, seek to regroup or restore emotional balance and well-being. Work during this phase includes identifying one's emotions, which may include embarrassment, shame, guilt, dejection, frustration, and anger. Just as naming the failure is important, naming our emotions can also help reduce the intensity of the feelings, and increased clarity can help us regain our balance. Following the model developed by Newton and colleagues (2008), we are wise to reflect and invite feedback from others to explore internal and external factors that contributed to the failure. In addition, we return to the balcony (Heifetz & Linksy, 2002) and remind ourselves that the failure is part of a larger teaching career filled with ups and downs, other failures, and successes.

*Learn.* Finally, we seek to learn from the experience. People who operate from a learning orientation are more likely to successfully navigate failure experiences (Newton et al., 2008). In this way, as educators who constantly seek to improve our craft, we are primed to grow from the experience. Reviewing the literature, Newton and colleagues (2008) found three categories of learning in executives who experienced failure: "stronger and more resilient sense of self and self-worth; stronger commitment to fundamental personal values and attitudes; and enhancement of specific competencies" (p. 239).

These growth areas are equally relevant in the faculty domain. Faculty tend to overestimate our role and power in the learning space (Brookfield, 2017), and so we are wise to follow failure with a recalibration of our sense of what is our responsibility and what is our students'.

Brookfield (2017) warns us against what he calls self-laceration or blaming ourselves exclusively when "students seem not to be learning" (p. 86). He says, "These teachers (and I'm one of them) feel that at some level, they're the cause of the anger, hostility, resentment, or indifference that even the best and most energetic of them are bound to encounter from time to time" (p. 86). Brookfield suggests that this mind-set leads faculty to overestimate their role in the learning space, believing that everything that happens—good, bad, and in between—is created, inspired, and delivered by the teacher.

In addition, some faculty, in their passion and commitment for teaching and learning, overfunction in their work with students. More than once I have realized that I was so engaged in trying to help a student learn or succeed, I was working harder than they were—this realization calls for self-evaluation and recalibration. Failure prompts us to go to the balcony and review our assumptions, expectations, commitments, and identity as teachers—a valuable check-in throughout one's career.

Newton and her colleagues (2008) also suggest that failure prompts people to reflect on and recommit to personal values. Failure can shift our perspective on work and remind us to spend more time with family and friends, attend to our health, and have fun. Academic life is fraught with never-ending work and persistent imbalance. While failure is hard precisely because it can be painful, the pain can also interrupt a default mode of saying yes far too often to requests from administration, colleagues, and even students—of taking on more than we should. Once our routine and momentum are interrupted, we may realize that our decisions and investments of time, energy, and gifts are misaligned with our values. Failure can prompt life-changing reprioritization.

Fortunately, the teaching life and the academic calendar also afford us the opportunity to revise our approaches, practices, and systems as we seek to learn from failure and improve. Failure can illuminate blind spots in our sense of self and skills (Newton et al., 2008) and flaws in our choice of materials, learning designs, and institutional systems and policies. For example, in transitioning a campus-based course to an online format, an instructor, after feeling that the course transition failed, might see a deficiency in his technical skills, a flaw in module designs, and gaps in the university's help desk support for students during evenings and weekends. Seeking training, redesigning the modules, and lobbying for expanded help desk hours would all be positive steps after the fraught semester. These changes, like the failure itself, may not be entirely in the instructor's control; for example, technology training may be limited or the administration may decline to expand help desk availability. Nonetheless, learning from failure and resulting clarity can lead to a more precise sense of where we as teachers can improve and adjust and which factors are outside our control.

While many people blame themselves for workplace failures, situational factors may also play a role. Newton and her colleagues (2008) identified a number of factors in a business setting that contribute to failure. Comparable factors in teaching might include structural changes such as increased teaching and advising loads, declining levels of preparation and ability of admitted students, budget cuts and loss of resources, and unstable or inefficient technology. We are wise to remember that occasional workplace failure is inevitable, and some elements that contribute to failure are beyond our control, regardless of our strengths and competencies (Newton et al., 2008).

## *Letting Go*

Even as we move through such a model, we may still find ourselves demoralized. In my own experience, although I grew from the failure and felt cognitively ready to move on, the hurt lingered. The various frameworks applied in this chapter—impasse, downward spiral, loss, failure, and the psychological contract—helped me better understand the experience and name some of the lived and residual emotion, but I felt there was some other uniden-tified quality to the experience. A colleague suggested that perhaps I felt wounded—this resonated somewhat. However, "wounded" also conjured images of paralysis and helplessness, which did not ring true. Wrestling with the language, I finally found resonance in thinking of the experience as an injury. Part of the hurt was likely the bruising of efficacy, identity, and pas-sion described earlier in this chapter. I understand now that to approach teaching from a relational perspective is to risk—to open oneself to deep disappointment and failure, which can be a source of social pain, a form of injury. I suspect that in these situations, students may feel similarly hurt.

Matthew Lieberman, his wife Naomi Eisenberger, and their colleagues are among the scholars using frontal magnetic resonance imaging (fMRI) to study the brain. They found that social pain—the experience of exclusion or rejection—activates the dorsal anterior cingulate cortex (dACC), which is the same part of the brain that is activated when we experience physical pain. Just as physical pain tells us to move to safety, so does social pain, indi-cating social connection is as important to our survival as is physical safety (Lieberman, 2014). Our bodies experience social pain much in the same way we experience physical pain—this is conceptualized as Social Pain Overlap Theory (SPOT) and was discovered via the Cyberball Studies (Lieberman, 2014).

Thinking of the experience as an injury makes so much sense. I was hurt, and yet like an injured athlete, I played on and expected no less of myself. As I taught through pain, the downward spiral continued, and the pain got more intense. For those of us who believe relationship is central to teaching, this kind of profound rupture in relationship with a group of stu-dents causes a tremendous sense of disconnection, the social pain described by Lieberman (2014).

Drawing on the Cyberball Studies (in which participants experienced being excluded from a video game of catch) and SPOT, I realize that at the end of the referred-to semester I felt separate from my students in a way I had not experienced previously in my teaching career. Not all of the individual relationships fell apart, but the tension in the classroom was severe at times, and the overall feelings between the class and me were strained. I would not say I felt excluded, because I still ran the class and had much of the power that comes with the position. But I often feel as if we are all in it together, and in this case, I felt deeply disconnected from these students; nothing could bridge the relational gap between us.

Viewing the experience as an injury reminded me it would take time to heal, but that I would heal, and this gave me hope as I began the next semes-ter. I started to regain my footing in subsequent meetings with students (not because we talked about the difficult semester but because I could once again see myself as effective and felt reconnected with students and teaching). I got back in the game and saw my potential and the promise of connected teaching once again.

Just as we seek to learn from and resolve these difficult teaching experiences, so too can we take preemptive measures, trying to prevent future ruptures or at least lessen their magnitude.

## Preemptive Measures

To accept failure as an inevitability of engaged dynamic teaching is to understand complexity and concede we do not have full control over the teaching and learning endeavor. Nonetheless, five strategies help us prepare for potential disappointment and failure: care for self and others, accept our fallibility and that of others, make the psychological contract visible, recognize and resist the relational paradox, and build and nourish relationships.

### *Care for Self and Others*

Brookfield (2015) claims that if we do not take care of ourselves, we cannot take care of others. Describing teaching as both a roller coaster and a roiling sea, Brookfield reminds us the teaching endeavor is full of peaks and valleys, sharp turns, and fear and exhilaration. An exploration of all that is involved in self-care is beyond the scope of this book, but as we know, rest, nutrition, movement, and relationships all play a role. Ongoing commitments to self-care help keep us steadier for the ups and downs of teaching, and go-to strategies for self-care are even more important in times of crisis.

### *Accept Our Fallibility*

Adding to Brookfield's (2015) suggestion that as teachers we may overestimate our role and influence, Daloz, Keen, Keen, and Parks (1996) proposed that shadow or taboo motivations can distort our sense of agency. These human qualities may include ambition, pride, perfectionism, need for control, need to please or be needed, guilt, and fear (Daloz et al., 1996). In addition, I suggest the teaching endeavor draws on additional essentially human motivations, including a wish to be liked (Palmer, 1998) and a need to be seen as competent.

Daloz and colleagues (1996) proposed that as we live lives of commitment, we are wise to remain alert to our shadow motivations and human limitations and to see them as "inevitable, though not debilitating" (p. 178). Those "who are able to sustain long-term work on behalf of the whole human family, it would seem, are full participants in the drama of human potential—and fallibility" (p. 178).

## Make the Psychological Contract Visible

This strategy will seem more at home in the social sciences and professions; however, it can be applied across disciplines. By teaching students about the psychological contract, we give them a framework with which to understand their own and our potential frustration in the teaching–learning journey. And we give them and ourselves a common language to discuss frustration or disillusionment should such feelings arise.

In addition, educating students about the psychological contract and asking them to reflect on and make known their expectations of themselves, while also sharing our implicit expectations of ourselves and students, can help avoid abuses of power on both sides. Teaching with transparency, we share power in the learning space. And perhaps students who clearly understand expectations that often go unspoken will be less likely to flex their power by refusing to work, consulting a dean, or venting their anger on the course evaluation.

Finally, by teaching students about the psychological contract, we give them a framework through which they can understand their own workplace disillusionment and thereby gain clarity in current or future employment. Working students may be able to provide examples in a related discussion, and faculty teaching classes wherein most students do not have work experience may employ a case study to examine the existence and effects of the psychological contract.

## Recognize and Resist the Relational Paradox

As suggested, many people tend to withdraw in times of trouble, believing they should go it alone, feeling embarrassed by their limitations, or seeking to prevent further social pain. The tendency to move away from relationship can contribute to the kind of downward spiral between teacher and students described in this chapter. Recognizing this tendency and resisting the urge can position us to remain in connection with students and thus in dialogue regarding the work at hand. No doubt, we are sometimes wise to momentarily step away to clear our heads, but an effort to ultimately remain in connection and in dialogue may help prevent further alienation and deterioration of a problematic project or course.

## *Build and Nourish Relationships*

Aside from team teaching, much of the work of our profession is done in isolation from our colleagues. Collegial relationships can take a back seat to our daily work and goal pursuit. However, we are wise to engage in the mutuality and richness of good collegial connections. These relationships not only help keep us steady amidst routine ups and downs but also become even more important in times of disillusionment.

Brookfield (2017) and Robertson (1999b) suggested formalizing a process of support among colleagues, calling on faculty to create professional development groups. Like supervision groups in professions such as counseling and social work, such groups provide a confidential space in which faculty can review, learn from, and garner support regarding difficult teaching experiences.

Closing this chapter, I turn to the wisdom of Carol Kasworm (2008), who suggests "learning is an act of hope" (p. 27). And I proclaim, so too is teaching.

# 9

---

# INTELLECTUAL
# MATTERING, AKA I LIKE
# THE WAY YOU THINK

*It also made me feel really good that she seemed very interested personally in the
study from her own personal perspective; that she got excited about it and said,
"Wow, this is going to be great. We are going to get some really great information
here, some new things." So that made me feel good that she herself was excited
about it more on a personal level than simply as my—my instructor. —Maggie*
(Schwartz, 2013, n.p.)

Throughout this book, I refer to mattering as central to connected
teaching. To matter is to feel we have a place in others' lives and
our presence makes a difference to them (Rosenberg & McCullough,
1981). "Are we an object of another's concern, interest, or attention?"
(p. 163).

When students know their thinking and academic development matter
to us, they are more likely to feel connected to the program (Schlossberg,
1987, 1989; Schwartz, 2013). Furthermore, mattering helps students stay
motivated, develop confidence, and transition from receivers to cocreators of
knowledge (Schwartz, 2013). In addition, we as faculty benefit from knowing our thinking and commitments matter to our students (Karpouza &
Emvalotis, 2018; Schwartz, 2009; Schwartz & Holloway, 2017).

When I think back to my most important teachers and mentors, I realize
that feeling as if I mattered to them was a common thread in all the relationships. I might not have articulated the experiences that way at the time,
but part of what I found compelling was a sense that I was not just another
student passing through but that they saw me and recognized my aspirations
and potential. Each of these mentors seemed to see me for who I was and for

who I could become. Moreover, they met me with enthusiasm and I often had the sense they saw me as part of their lives too, that they thought of me between meetings or would go the extra mile to help me. Without these people, I am confident I would not be where I am today. I believe I would have succeeded in school and beyond, but I suspect I would not have progressed to where I am now. At key moments in my development, these mentors fueled my growth and accelerated my progress.

Likewise, upon reflection I realize some of my most memorable and motivating experiences as a teacher have been when I felt I mattered in the lives of students, I brought something important to their growth. When students take the time to tell us we have been helpful (and, even better, how we have been helpful), we are struck not only by their gratitude but also by the affirmation that we bring something significant to their lives. When we see students respond to a course activity or our feedback, we sense we make a difference, we matter.

Neuroscience affirms mattering's import—neurologically, we need to connect with others (Banks, 2015; Lieberman, 2014). According to Lieberman (2014),

> Being socially connected is a need with a capital *N*. . . . Love and belonging might seem like a convenience we can live without, but our biology is built to thirst for connection because it is linked to our most basic survival needs. (p. 43)

While mattering has been a touch point in several chapters in this book, this chapter provides a deeper explication of mattering, specifically intellectual mattering or "knowing that our thinking matters to another person" (Schwartz, 2013, abstract). This chapter begins with an overview of mattering and its converse—marginality. In the second half, I explore intellectual mattering.

## How Do We Know We Matter to Others?

Sensing we matter in the lives of others, that we are part of the social fabric, is essential to well-being, according to Rosenberg and McCullough (1981), who also noted that at its most basic, mattering is the opposite of passing through life fundamentally unnoticed by others. "The most elementary form of mattering is the feeling that one commands the interest or notice of another person. The only prospect more bleak than to die unmourned is to die unnoticed" (Rosenberg & McCullough, 1981, p. 164).

Rosenberg and McCullough are credited with introducing the concept of mattering, first presenting at the annual meeting of the American Sociological Association in 1979 and later publishing their first related paper in 1981. Their research suggests we know we matter when we are the object of others' attention, when we sense others care for us, and when others depend on us. Schlossberg (1989) later identified an additional element of mattering—appreciation.

## Attention

Attention in its most basic form is being noticed; do others respond to us in some basic way when we enter a room (Rosenberg & McCullough, 1981)? Connecting with students directly can be a challenge given back-to-back classes and otherwise busy schedules. However, when possible, I try to engage. When time permits, I attempt to connect briefly with each student before class—even a quick check-in, an inquiry as to their well-being, or follow-up if I can remember some particular from their reporting of the previous week (e.g., how was your daughter's birthday, or how did the interview go?). While this may seem like small talk, remembering even small details about students' lives conveys care and mattering by communicating I remember something about them, and they are in my thoughts. Students have occasionally commented to me or noted in their end-of-course evaluation that they find this gesture important.

I wonder about the impact of showing up and not feeling noticed or seen by others week after week. Might this deepen disconnection when students struggle with material or question fit with a program? Might students be more likely to disengage for academic or professional reasons when they already feel as if their coming and going does not matter to the professor and other students in the course? I do not mean to suggest a quick hello from a professor is a make-or-break element of academic success or even motivation. I believe students are generally propelled by deeper drives such as professional or personal goals. And first and foremost, students find and manifest their own motivation and discipline. However, perhaps being noticed and knowing others care that you showed up online or in the classroom occasionally tips the scale in favor of persevering past moments of doubt, frustration, or indifference.

## Feeling Important

Beyond feeling *noticed*, feeling *important* to another person is a more powerful sense of mattering. In the context of teaching and learning relationships, when we believe others care about our well-being, our progress, and our goals, we experience mattering. Relevant to our work as teachers, Rosenberg and McCullough (1981) suggested mattering can be separate from approval, so, as noted in chapter 4, students can sense they matter to us even when we are critical of their work, if they concurrently feel we care about their learning. And individualized critical feedback may in fact convey mattering more clearly than rote or shallow positive comment.

## Dependence (With a Twist)

Dependence is another indicator of mattering. The interesting and perhaps counterintuitive twist regarding dependence is that we know we matter not when we can depend on others but when we sense others depend on us. "Mattering represents a compelling social obligation and a powerful source of social integration: we are bonded to society not only by virtue of our dependence on others but by their dependence on us" (Rosenberg & McCullough, 1981, p. 165). Asking students for feedback on courses and the program, and when appropriate seeking their involvement in short-term or long-term collaborative projects, may convey mattering. I will describe students' import in our ongoing development as intellectual mattering and mutuality later in this chapter. Dependence in extremes, though, can cause distress. For example, adult students who feel that their partners, children, or aging family members depend on them extensively may have difficulty completing school and caring for self. And clearly there would be an imbalance if students sense we depend on them more than they can depend on us. So dependence is best experienced in moderation.

## Appreciation

On the basis of her research with adult students, Nancy Schlossberg (1989) added appreciation, an additional aspect of mattering. Students in Schlossberg's study indicated feeling they mattered when others acknowledged their effort. This notion might conjure images of participation trophies and related recognition that some see as hollow. However, I suggest that recognition of student effort can hold more substantial meaning, for both adult students and 18- to 22-year-olds.

Adult students often make significant sacrifices to engage in school, such as foregoing time with family and giving up any semblance of a personal life. Moreover, adults may manage significant responsibility in nonschool areas of life, such as work, parenting, and other caregiving, and yet receive little appreciation for their effort. Thus, having one's effort seen and recognized in the academic setting may be significant in sustaining adult students as they seek to balance family, work, and school. Knowing one's effort is appreciated in school may help adult students reaffirm their commitment amidst feeling overly depended upon at home. In addition, adult students who begin school later in adulthood, return after an earlier failure, or enroll in graduate work having been out of school for an extended period may wrestle with doubt and hit obstacles early in their journey, such as challenges with technology, academic writing, or statistics. Likewise, 18- to 22-year-old students are likely to appreciate when faculty notice their efforts. Like adult students, many 18- to 22-year-old students balance work and school, struggle with confidence, and look for cues that their educational and career goals are attainable.

## Marginality

Schlossberg (1989) further helps us consider mattering in the lives of college students as she discusses mattering alongside its converse experience—marginality. Schlossberg recognizes that sociocultural identity can contribute to feelings of being on the margin. She suggests, for example, bicultural people may not feel entirely at home in either distinct culture, and international students may struggle with attempting to fit in with American culture while remaining connected to their home country. Similarly, Lubrano (2005) writes powerfully about the experience of people who grow up in working-class or low-income contexts and then attend college and thus straddle class cultures throughout their lives. Social constructions of identity, as already discussed throughout this book, can lead to profound marginalization, as people of color, immigrants and refugees, LGBTQ people, and others receive messages daily (ranging from subtle to violent) that they do not belong.

Bullying, ridicule, shunning, and other forms of isolation cause profound social pain. As noted, social exclusion, or social pain, triggers neurological activity in the same part of the brain as does physical pain; social pain is real and increases the likelihood of depression, withdrawal, physical illness, and suicide (Lieberman, 2014; Sue & Sue, 2016). Letting students know they matter in school can even slightly counter society's messages of marginalization. Conveying to students they matter may give them a place where they feel valued rather than excluded.

Illustrating a less obvious yet significant experience of marginality, Schlossberg (1989) described the sense of being on the margins many people feel upon entering a new situation or in the midst of transition. A professor of 12 years when she wrote the article, Schlossberg recalled feeling important when she was on campus in general but marginal when entering a student dining area or attending a parent–teacher conference at her child's school. Echoing Rosenberg and McCullough (1981), she noted that when she engaged in the latter two situations and nobody said hello or acknowledged her presence, she questioned whether she belonged or mattered in the new context. She also described transitions as a distinct time when people struggle with feeling a sense of mattering or connection.

> Every time an individual changes roles or experiences a transition, the potential for feeling marginal arises. The larger the difference between the former role and the new role the more marginal the person may feel, especially if there are no norms for the new roles. The first students of nontraditional age to attend traditional campuses, for example, faced such problems. They had no norms to anticipate their pioneering role. (Schlossberg, 1989, p. 7)

Returning to my earlier point that acknowledging effort and other forms of mattering is far more than the equivalent of participation trophies, I propose mattering is a significant strategy of connected teaching. We convey to students we see them and care about their well-being and success, and this, in turn, can contribute to students' initial adjustment, persistence, increased confidence, and development of scholar-practitioner identity (Schwartz, 2013). And importantly, we can communicate mattering in concert with critical feedback, reminders about attendance and commitment, and other aspects of assessing student work.

Rosenberg and McCullough (1981) and Schlossberg (1987, 1989) have provided the foundation for my development of the concept of intellectual mattering. Several other scholars have studied mattering in higher education with various foci: first-generation undergraduate students (Stebleton, Soria, & Huesman, 2014), urban Latino male undergraduates (Huerta & Fishman, 2014), African American students at predominantly white institutions (Strayhorn, 2012), Black male students at a historically Black university (Palmer & Maramba, 2012), urban student populations (Tovar, Simon, & Lee, 2009), adult learners (MacKinnon-Slaney, 1994), mattering and stress among undergraduates (Dixon Rayle & Chung, 2008; Gibson & Myers, 2006; Myers & Bechtel, 2004), and generally over the course of undergraduate studies (Marshall, Liu, Wu, Berzonsky, & Adams, 2010).

## Intellectual Mattering

My understanding of intellectual mattering has continued to evolve since I first introduced the concept at the Sixth Annual Mentoring Conference at the University of New Mexico. My journey with this concept began after I had completed a few studies regarding meaningful interactions and relationships between faculty and students. Over time, I realized students sometimes discussed a particular kind of phenomenon with faculty. I realized some students described interactions as important not only when a professor complimented their work but also when they sensed their ideas or work were important to the professor. I began the first article on intellectual mattering by claiming "students notice when we notice" (Schwartz, 2013, p. 1). Given this was about the students' thinking and ideas, I named the concept "intellectual mattering." Beginning to develop a related presentation, I searched the literature and found the concept of mattering was already established, thus affirming my conceptualization of this aspect of connected teaching.

After engaging with the extant mattering literature, I returned to the data from my earlier studies that had initially sparked the idea. Reviewing the data, I ascertained that students described two types of intellectual mattering: content oriented and process oriented. I have continued to sustain and develop these ideas through additional research and critical conversations with colleagues. Later in this section I describe the import of authenticity and power as relevant to intellectual mattering.

*Content mattering.* Students experience mattering when they sense their ideas or thoughts have touched or affected their teacher (Schwartz, 2013; Schwartz & Holloway, 2014). The story at the beginning of this chapter reveals content mattering. The student senses her professor is excited about her research idea. Notice the professor says, "We are going to get some really great information here, some new things"; by saying "we," the professor indicates she too will learn from working with the student and that the student's research idea could contribute to her own learning. In addition, the student notes the professor was "excited about it more on a personal level than simply as my—my instructor." Here the student echoes my claim in chapter 2 that students make a distinction between interactions that are "part of the job" and those that are above and beyond, the latter indicating more care and personal commitment to the student.

Students also sense their thinking matters to their professors when they realize their professors think of them beyond the classroom.

> *I had one professor who was introducing me to his wife and daughter and had said some words about a presentation I had done in his class or something, so just the fact that they remember those things and you realize that they're sharing their in-class experiences with their families as much as we are sometimes, so fortunately, it increased my, I guess, my level of connection with those professors.*
> —Dawn (Schwartz & Holloway, 2014, p. 47)

*Process mattering.* Meaningful and purposeful engagement also conveys mattering to students. Again, this echoes the claims in chapter 2 regarding meaningful interactions. The difference between content and process mattering is subtle because both are conveyed by faculty and relate to student progress and work. Process mattering, another way to understand meaningful single interactions, is expressed through actions and time shared with students:

> She met me early in the morning before I had to go to work, and you know on this—you know, eraser board—laid out every element of what my paper was, and it was a day that she didn't have to be there; she came in specially to meet with me, and she took—you know, an hour out of her time. And we talked about the paper, and she helped me . . . all the elements of my paper were there, I just had them all wrong, and so just seeing them on the board we were able to move things around. And then I don't know, she was just encouraging me.
> —Rebecca (Schwartz, 2009, p. 91)

When we offer to stay after class or engage in a one-on-one video call with a student to review a paper, clarify a confusing concept, or discuss research ideas or future plans, students may perceive, through the gesture or action alone, that we care, they matter to us. Likewise, when we send students extra readings based on a topic they raise in class or help them make a networking contact, they also sense they matter to us, we see their potential and want to help them grow.

### Benefits of Intellectual Mattering

Students who believe they matter in the lives of their professors experience a boost of energy and self-worth and may shift from passive to active learning. This progression is vital for student engagement and helping students develop a scholar-practitioner identity (Karpouza & Emvalotis, 2018; Schwartz, 2013; Schwartz & Holloway, 2014). Revealing a shift in mind-set that I believe we wish for all students, one study participant recalled,

> I became a part of the learning process. I take more ownership of what I'm being able to learn because I was able to relate to this professor and I was able to build more of a relationship. I'm able to communicate with the professor and I'm able to engage, and I'm able to learn. I'm able to learn versus just being taught, or just going in—I'm paying you so you can give me information versus, no, I need to learn and I need to be engaged. —Rebecca (Schwartz & Holloway, 2014, p. 50)

In this student reflection, we also see evidence that relational teaching reinforces possible selves, as discussed in chapter 4. Through a good connection with a professor, this student is affirmed in her development. Intellectual mattering is a motivational force; "students who believe that they matter connect with their aspirational possible selves and are motivated to achieve" (Schwartz, 2013, n.p.). The following student story reflects the transformational power of these moments.

> *He pushed me to the next level, you know? And so it was—that was a real turn in a lot of ways, and then I could ask more educated questions, you know, I could—I could—you know instead of just going "what is this theoretical model" . . . we can have a more intelligent conversation about the topic beyond—so what is this thing. You know so it—it just—it was one of those real stepping off points for me. —Maria* (Schwartz, 2013, n.p.)

## Authenticity Is Essential

When we seek to convey intellectual mattering, we must do so with authenticity; only when we are authentic will students trust our words, and this trustworthiness gives expressions of mattering their credence and value. "The idea is not to look for opportunities to deliver compliments, but rather to recognize those moments when we are truly touched, informed, motivated, or inspired by a student's work and then to intentionally share our response with that student" (Schwartz, 2013, n.p.). Authenticity establishes trustworthiness, and this is essential in the teacher–student relationship (Brookfield, 2006). Cranton and Carusetta (2004) identified five dimensions of authenticity: awareness of self, awareness of students, relationships with students, contextual awareness, and engagement in critical reflection on practice. Cranton and Carusetta's work reinforces that expressions of intellectual mattering emerge from awareness. When we are aware of ourselves and our students, as well as the context in which we teach and the larger cultural context, we are positioned to be open to and struck by student thinking; we are then able to notice when we are moved or influenced. Self-awareness regarding position, power, and relational clarity in general situates us to tell students their thinking has influenced us, an inherently power-with move.

## Intellectual Mattering as Power-With

When we convey to students their thinking matters, and their ideas have influenced or inspired us, we reduce the hierarchy in the relationship. To acknowledge we can learn from students or be moved by their work is to recognize we are still learning and can be influenced even by students who might be thought of as junior or emerging scholar-practitioners. As discussed in chapter 6, when we let go of the mystique of the intellectually superior professor, we share power with our students. This move is fully consistent with Relational-Cultural Theory (RCT) and also echoes Cranton and Carusetta's (2004) call to know ourselves, students, teaching contexts, and relationships and to engage in practice critically. To remain secure in ourselves as we share our power, we must know ourselves, know where our power or authority resides, and then reflect critically to remain clear in our role responsibilities as students strengthen their confidence and position in the teaching relationship. Novice teachers who struggle with feeling secure in their role may have trouble sharing power in this way, as would any teacher who relies on or enjoys a power-over position.

## Intellectual Mattering: More Than the Meeting of Two Minds

As I discussed intellectual mattering with RCT founding scholar Judith V. Jordan, attempting to discern the difference between this concept and intimacy in teaching, which I will consider in the conclusion, Jordan helped me see that as I have described intellectual mattering up to this point, it may seem to be primarily a cognitive connection. This makes sense because the concept, both in content and in process manifestations, is centered on recognizing the importance of another person's thinking. While intellectual mattering is largely connected to one's thoughts, ideas, and interests, it is the emotional energy of the ideas themselves and the mattering they generate that add significantly to their richness and centrality in our lives.

Working on this book is inherently stimulating; however, the notion of sharing these ideas makes them come alive. Imagining these ideas will help others think about their teaching motivates me throughout the writing and revision process. I think about how this applies to students. I wonder if when students feel disconnected in an online learning environment, they feel as if their presence does not matter. Certainly, their work gets assessed by faculty, and they may engage with classmates in a dialogue group or discussion board. However, I wonder if online courses with minimal interaction cause some students to feel disconnected, which may be discouraging to all but the most driven and disciplined students. I wonder if feeling as if they do not matter in the learning space is actually a more nuanced understanding of feelings of disconnection that discourage some students from online learning. Of course, not all online learning is disconnected, and some faculty who teach online skillfully create community and a sense of belonging. Furthermore, connection does not matter to all students who engage in online learning. Nonetheless, I know many students who avoid or eventually try online learning and then in the future avoid such courses. Perhaps the lack of connection leaves them feeling as if their presence is not important, and this diminishes energy.

Miller and Stiver's earliest work might provide help as we seek to understand the emotional richness of intellectual mattering. Miller and Stiver (1997) challenged the typically Western split between thoughts and emotions. "It is significant that there does not seem to be a common word in our language to convey the concept of 'feeling-thoughts' or 'thought-feelings'—that is, thoughts together with their accompanying emotions" (Miller & Stiver, 1997, p. 27). They attribute the division to the gendering of our culture, proposing that thinking is valued and seen as male and feeling is devalued and seen as female. "In contrast, we believe that all thoughts are accompanied by emotions and all emotions have a thought content. Attempting to focus on one to the neglect of the other diminishes people's ability to understand and act on their experience" (Miller & Stiver, 1997, p. 212).

Perhaps in naming the concept *intellectual mattering*, the intellectual component has overwhelmed the mattering—has the cognitive taken on more prominence than the emotion? When I think about the student stories that stirred this idea of intellectual mattering, I am struck by the joy or pride the students convey. When I reflect on times when I think my thinking mattered to a peer, student, or teacher, the emotional memory is stronger than and connected with the thought memory (though this distinction is false as they are interwoven).

Cavanagh (2016) argues teaching has typically been considered a serious endeavor with little room for emotion, but in fact learning and emotion are deeply connected.

> Increasingly, neuroscience research indicates that the brain systems involved in emotion and those involved in cognition are not, as traditional accounts would have us believe, separate systems pulling us in opposite directions. Rather . . . overlapping circuits are responsible for both, and the biochemical bases for each are very similar. (p. 3)

An evolutionary force, emotions drive motivation—pushing us to take actions (e.g., eating) that support survival and to avoid actions (e.g., stepping off a cliff or into fire) that would lead to our demise (Cavanagh, 2016). Emotions "also influence learning—tagging certain experiences and skills as important and thus critical to both attend to and remember" (Cavanagh, 2016, p. 3). Perhaps emotions *label* experiences and skills (and information) as important, but in addition moments and learning *become* important because of the attached emotion.

In my previous examples of intellectual mattering, we can see emotions tagging experiences as important when Maria feels challenged by her professor and wants to do her best. Likewise, Dawn remembers a moment as important because her professor acknowledged her work to his family. This acknowledgment, at least in her retelling, was specifically related not to the content of her work but to his recognition of her to his family, in which he is indicating she matters. Sure, he was discussing her work, but what she seems left with is she matters to her teacher, and thus we can surmise she is a valued part of the academic community, she is part of the social fabric of this world she chose to enter. Conceivably, intellectual mattering provides an additional link between affect and cognition, signaling the emotional experience of belonging, of being important in the social world of one's program, department, or school, and this holds significance for both students and teachers.

Social connection's importance in the teaching and learning context is essential—feeling connected to others is critical in the human experience, and this is proclaimed by both RCT and neuroscience. Perhaps this is at the heart of connected teaching. When your thinking matters to me, you matter to me, and when my thinking matters to you, I matter to you. And thus, intellectual mattering conveyed through content and process becomes foundational in the social world of teaching and learning. Intellectual mattering, more than just knowing one's thinking matters to another, may be about knowing we matter to each other as teachers and students. Knowing we matter may be yet another manifestation of belonging and connection as essential in the human experience, crucial for our survival. I submit that when we convey intellectual mattering to our students, we manifest Daloz's (1999) call to welcome them to a new world.

## Intellectual Mattering in Faculty Life

Just as intellectual mattering is important in student lives, so it is in our lives too (Karpouza & Emvalotis, 2018). Holloway (2017), recalls her work with a dissertating student. She remembers a video call that was pivotal for the student and meaningful for her as well:

> This student stops herself from acknowledging her capacity. She had her findings, and she said, "How can I possibly make sense of all of this?" And I said, "Talk me through what you know." I took out paper and pencil and sketched my visual understanding of her meaning making of the data. I

held it up to the camera and showed it to her and she said, "Oh my, I have no idea how you do that." I said, "We all have different ways of knowing, I see it first visually and then translate into text. You see first in words and so you offered that to me." I've subsequently been involved in and have seen the visual representations of her findings in her dissertation and I know that moment of working with her connects me with my involvement and joy in her work. (Holloway, September 29, 2017)

This example reflects attention, feeling important, dependence, and appreciation—the elements of mattering (Rosenberg & McCullough, 1981; Schlossberg, 1987, 1989). Holloway experiences herself as important to the student, who depends on and appreciates her.

As her thinking joined with the student's, they made sense of the data together. Holloway recalled seeing the final visualizations of the student's work and sensing the impact of their earlier conversations and her contribution to the student's ability to make meaning. The memory is not simply about the student's intellectual growth or Holloway's role but also about the moment of connection when they thought together, when together they explored the findings.

Moreover, in this memory, Holloway recalls being moved by the student's noticing; she remembers the student's words, "I have no idea how you do that," a moment in which Holloway's strength as a conceptual thinker is recognized by the student. In the student's exuberance, she conveyed something fundamental: Holloway's place as a teacher in the life of a student matters. In that moment, Holloway's mattering is not cursory but profound—she matters to another through the expression and enactment of her life's work.

In the following quote, Holloway describes both the nuance of her work-in-relation and the profound meaning of shared dialogue-in-connection. Holloway's approach reflects authenticity and relational clarity:

It reminds me of our different capacities and the delicate balance of offering up that which I see and not overtaking the project. It's this dance of dialogue that allows both to lead toward a deeper understanding of the findings. That experience, that dialogue, the dialogue that happens in a built relationship of teaching and learning, that shared space of conceptual turbulence lays ground for creative convergence. It is these moments that exhilarate me as a mentor and a researcher. (Holloway, September 29, 2017)

According to Holloway, the dialogue is powerful not only for its intellectual content but also because it happens in "a built relationship of teaching and learning." Her perception that the shared space holds the conceptual turbulence such that she and the student can work together creatively echoes Heifetz and Linksy's (2002) suggestion of the holding space. And again, her realization that these moments "exhilarate her as a mentor and a researcher" evidence the power and mutuality of connected teaching. Holloway's story sets the stage for this book's conclusion, in which we explore intimacy and teaching.

## CONCLUSION

# A LIFE'S WORK

A midst all the other experiences in a teacher's life, there are those occasional moments of meaningful connection with students. To some
degree, all of my searching throughout this book—my quest to better understand when teaching goes right and when it goes wrong, when we
connect and when we feel disconnected—is about these moments, when
together with students, we strive.

So much of our work is intangible. We hope students learn, and sometimes we think they do. At the end of a given semester, their papers, pres-
entations, exams, or dissertations provide evidence. These representations of
student learning are important, and we may feel satisfied or impressed as we
review student work. But seeing students learn, being with students in the
moment of learning—these moments are profound. I remain frustrated there
is no word for this kind of deep engagement—of learning, creating, and
becoming with another. In her chapter titled "Mutuality and Resonance,"
Josselson (1995) writes,

> Mutuality occurs *between* selves and this is part of why language falters.
> Anyone who has seriously addressed this space between loses articulate-
> ness and begins to create hyphenated words (Miller, 1986). Thus Buber
> creates the "I-Thou" (1958), Miller speaks of the "self-in-relation," and
> Stern (1985) postulates a state of "being with." Because our language
> tends to make assignments to me or you, we lack the discourse of we.
> (p. 148)

We lack language for the space between, the energy between. I see this
as a kind of *intimacy* but have struggled with using the word in this context,
fearing its popular connotations of romance and sex might distract from and
confuse what I am trying to explain.

However, when we consider the etymology of *intimate* we come closer.
*Intimate* has its roots in the Latin *intimus*, translated as "inmost," and *inti-
mare*, to "impress, make familiar" (Intimate, n.d.). In these intense moments

of teaching and learning, we and our students bring ourselves—our intellect, emotions, identities, and physicality—to the encounter. We join in this exclusive yet elusive space of connection and discovery. In these richest of teaching encounters, we simultaneously bring our inmost, or innermost, selves, and through our work together we discover (make familiar) something new.

Initially, I thought of this nascent space between as a meeting of our best selves. But I am not always my best self with students—sometimes I am tired or fighting irritability. And students are not always their best selves either. In these ways, we bring our most human selves. Our imperfection is our humanity, and we aspire to do better. We and our students arrive not knowing all there is to know—we bring our aspirational selves.

The teaching space is a space in which vulnerability and doubt are potential. I intend to do my best work, and students intend to learn. Thus, I am bringing a fundamental part of myself to the interaction, the part who has chosen to be a teacher. And students bring a vital part of themselves, the part who has chosen to be a student. For us, this is our life's work. For students, this may represent the drive to get a needed degree, passion for the discipline, or a longtime, closely held personal goal. Regardless, we do not bring our trivial selves; we bring our essential selves. The stakes are high.

As we, teacher and student, begin this interaction, we are poised for something to happen (Walker, 2004). Perhaps we and our students enter the moment in paradox—clinging to who we are and simultaneously eager for who we might become. In the exchange, I hope by bringing the best authentic presence I can muster, I will engage, support, and challenge *the person before me*—both the student sitting in front of me and the person I was before.

Moreover, there is something essential about learning in connection as different from learning alone. When we learn together, we share not only the content of our disciplines but also the energy and emotion of the learning moment. We are part of the world! Miller and Stiver (1997) described this as being "in the flow of human connection" (p. 35). Flow (Csikszentmihalyi, 2008) is a robust state—we are intrinsically motivated and present, we create and achieve, we thrive, and we are fully alive.

If, as Buber (1958) suggests, "all real living is meeting" (p. 11), then each of these meetings or interactions builds a life. Jordan (2004) proposes that "the yearning for and movement toward connection are seen as central organizing factors in people's lives" (p. 11). Just as we move toward connection, connection moves us and our students. The richness of these exchanges lies not only in the learned content or clarified career goal but also as confirmation that we have the capacity to move and be moved—we matter.

> In the course of life, each person builds a basic inner sense of his or her ability to act—of empowerment—as a result of the experience of seeing that he or she can have an impact on others. This means, of course, that we also acquire more ability to act because of other people's response to us—their impact on us. (Miller & Stiver, 1997, p. 36)

So each connection, whether a single interaction or a long-term relationship, builds our capacity to teach and learn, to grow into our potential.

This is magnified in the lineage of students who become teachers. Often, at least some of our motivation to teach was ignited by consequential interactions we experienced as students with our teachers and mentors. They illuminated our potential, and we yearn to do the same for others. We felt the intimacy of connection—manifest in the spark of possibility and the fire of shared discovery. We crave more of this feeling and aspire to experience it from the other side of the desk.

We know we want to change the world, and through our teacher-mentors we begin to believe we can. In these most powerful connections, we came to learn, and we left changed. With teacher-mentors, we transform in ways we had not imagined.

> As we grow we come to realize that their gift is not the opportunity to become *like* them, but the challenge to become more fully ourselves *through* them. They call for the best we have. They invite us to transcend ourselves. They embody our deep aspirations. (Daloz, 1999, pp. 224–225)

We want to give something back to these all-important people, and yet deep down we know we have nothing to offer them that would near the magnitude of what they have done for us. So we do our best to express gratitude and commit to passing it on. Driven by all we have learned about our disciplines, ourselves, and the world, we yearn to help others feel something of what we felt as we came into our own, as we came to see our innermost selves as people who could contribute something to the world.

And so, we teach. We connect with students from the other side of the literal or metaphorical desk. In connection, we begin anew, each of us knowing less than we will and growing more than we thought possible. In connection, we create something bigger than ourselves.

In connection, we become.

# AFTERWORD

In *Connected Teaching*, Harriet L. Schwartz brings together several emerging educational and psychological perspectives. She guides us, with humility and conviction, toward creating a pedagogy informed by the power of relationship. In so doing, she contributes to an essential shift in our understanding of how best to engage in education.

Relational-Cultural Theory (RCT) suggests that we grow through and toward relationship throughout our life span. In the RCT model of growth, there is an emphasis on mutuality. As Jean Baker Miller said, "If in a relationship both people aren't growing, neither person is growing." Faculty are not performing their role in order to grow, *to gain* something from the student or the situation. But in real connection, both people are changed. Teachers occupy a role, and they are accountable for bringing intentionality to the student–teacher relationship. They are responsible for making sure that risks taken are not too ambitious and for following through on the inevitable disconnects and failures that occur. Faculty are the shepherds of growth and relational well-being in academia.

While providing a positive model for education, Schwartz also includes helpful analyses of some of the tough spots in teaching. What happens when the teacher feels like a failure or does not enjoy the excitement of watching a student "get" some previously elusive idea? What about when the teacher feels dismissed or attacked? Schwartz advocates for nondefensively taking in the feedback, pausing, inviting collaborative exploration of such triggering events. We aim for responsiveness, not reactivity.

There is a distinct power difference in the professor–student dyad. How can teachers use power differentials in such a way that the student is empowered rather than endangered? Transparency and naming of the power dynamics is essential. It does no one a favor in a power-stratified relationship to pretend that such an imbalance does not exist.

Schwartz addresses the importance of *mattering*, which is often related to power. Who matters in this relationship? When students know that we are interested in them, care about their well-being, think about them, and remember details of conversation, the power imbalance becomes less endangering. When we convey that their feelings, their goals, and their struggles matter to us, they can begin to settle in to trust and hope.

Bringing in recent developments in neuroscience, Schwartz points out the ways in which our brains are primed to connect and to grow through connection. In exploring sociopolitical aspects of connected teaching, Schwartz looks at the impact of inequality, marginalization, and exclusion. She cautions us to bring awareness to privilege, difference, and oppression as they arise in the classroom. Both the macro and micro aspects of connected teaching are explored.

Schwartz imparts that she holds a "feisty optimism" (p. 115, this volume) and a deep belief in the power of connected teaching. Acknowledging her own shortcomings, limits, and uncertainties, alongside her devotion to her students, she remains present and accessible. With gentle humor and openness, often joining with her students, she models a path of humility, curiosity, confidence, and the real strength of those who can explore uncertainty and imperfection.

This is a highly intelligent book, anchored in feeling and relationship. The timing of this exploration is exquisite. We are living in an era of isolation, despair, failing trust. It is reassuring that Schwartz, with her feisty optimism, is determined to bring a relational–cultural understanding to bear on our educational challenges.

We have been led to believe that individual achievement, exercising power over others, and emphasizing the need for solitary action will bring fulfillment and happiness. I disagree. We are, as some bumper stickers now proclaim, "stronger together." Rather than only fortifying the individual, we need to expand our dedication to the common good. To quote Schwartz, "In connection, we create something bigger than ourselves" (p. 147, this volume). This book is a beacon, guiding us to appreciate the significance of mutual learning and an expanding sense of human possibility—hope.

Judith V. Jordan
Director, Jean Baker Miller Training Institute
Founding Scholar, Relational-Cultural Theory
Assistant Professor of Psychiatry, Harvard Medical School

# REFERENCES

1.7.2 Consensual sexual or romantic relationships in the workplace and educational setting. (2017, November 21). Stanford University. Retrieved from https://adminguide.stanford.edu/chapter-1/subchapter-7/policy-1-7-2

Albers, C. (2009). Teaching: From disappointment to ecstasy. *Teaching Sociology, 37*(3), 269–282.

Banks, A. (2015). *Four ways to click: Rewire your brain for stronger, more rewarding relationships.* New York, NY: Tarcher/Penguin.

Barnett, J. E. (2008). Mentoring, boundaries, and multiple relationships: Opportunities and challenges. *Mentoring & Tutoring: Partnership in Learning, 16*(1), 3–16.

Belenky, M. F., Clinchy, B. M., Goldberger, N. R., & Tarule, J. M. (1997). *Women's ways of knowing: The development of self, voice, and mind* (10th anniversary ed.). New York, NY: Basic Books.

Belenky, M. F., & Stanton, A. V. (2000). Inequality, development, and connected knowing. In J. Merzirow & Associates (Eds.), *Learning as transformation: Critical perspectives on a theory in progress* (pp. 71–102). San Francisco, CA: Jossey-Bass.

Berg, M., & Seeber, B. K. (2017). *The slow professor: Challenging the culture of speed in the academy.* Toronto, Canada: University of Toronto Press.

Berk, R. A. (1996). Student ratings of 10 strategies for using humor in college teaching. *Journal on Excellence in College Teaching, 7*(3), 71–92.

Booth, M., & Schwartz, H. L. (2012). We're all adults here: Clarifying and maintaining boundaries with adult learners. *New Directions for Teaching and Learning, 2012*(131), 43–55.

Bordia, S., Hobman, E. V., Restubog, S. L., & Bordia, P. (2010). Advisor–student relationship in business project collaborations: A psychological contract perspective. *Journal of Applied Social Psychology, 40*(9), 2360–2386.

Boring, A., Ottoboni, K., & Stark, P. B. (2016, January). Student evaluations of teaching (mostly) do not measure teaching effectiveness. *ScienceOpen Research,* 1–11.

boyd, d. (2002). *FACETED ID/ENTITY: Managing representation in a digital world* (Master's thesis). Retrieved from http://www.danah.org/papers/Thesis.Faceted Identity.pdf

Brandeis University. (2012, May 24). *Policy on faculty and staff relations with students.* Retrieved from http://www.brandeis.edu/provost/faculty-info/pdfs/faculty_staff_relations_with_students_policy.pdf

Brookfield, S. (1984). *Adult learners, adult education and the community.* Berkshire, UK: Open University Press.

Brookfield, S. D. (1995). *Becoming a critically reflective teacher.* San Francisco, CA: Jossey-Bass.

Brookfield, S. D. (2006). Authenticity and power. *New Directions for Adult and Continuing Education, 2006*(111), 5–16.

Brookfield, S. D. (2015). *The skillful teacher: On technique, trust, and responsiveness in the classroom.* San Francisco, CA: Jossey-Bass.

Brookfield, S. D. (2017). *Becoming a critically reflective teacher* (2nd ed.). San Francisco, CA: Jossey-Bass.

Brown, B. C. (2012). *Daring greatly: How the courage to be vulnerable transforms the way we live, love, parent, and lead.* New York, NY: Gotham Books.

Buber, M. (1958). *I and thou.* New York, NY: Charles Scribner's Sons.

Buck, G. A., Mast, C. M., Latta, M. A. M., & Kaftan, J. M. (2009). Fostering a theoretical and practical understanding of teaching as a relational process: A feminist participatory study of mentoring a doctoral student. *Educational Action Research, 17*(4), 505–521.

California Newsreel. (2003). *Race: The power of an illusion* [Documentary film]. United States: California Newsreel.

Cavanagh, S. R. (2016). *The spark of learning: Energizing the college classroom with the science of emotion.* Morgantown, WV: West Virginia University Press.

Charron, K. M. (2009). *Freedom's teacher: The life of Septima Clark.* Chapel Hill, NC: University of North Carolina Press.

Collins, P. H. (1993). Toward a new vision: Race, class, and gender as categories of analysis and connection. *Race, Sex & Class,* 25–45.

Collins, P. H. (1999). *Black feminist thought: Knowledge, consciousness, and the politics of empowerment* (2nd ed.). New York, NY: Routledge.

Consensual Relationships. (2017, January 3). University of Texas at Austin. Retrieved from https://policies.utexas.edu/policies/consensual-relationships

Cranton, P., & Carusetta, E. (2004). Perspectives on authenticity in teaching. *Adult Educational Quarterly, 55*(5), 5–22.

Cress, C. M. (2008). Creating inclusive learning communities: The role of student–faculty relationships in mitigating negative campus climate. *Learning Inquiry, 2*(2), 95–111.

Cross, P. K. (1981). *Adults as learners: Increasing participation and facilitating learning.* San Francisco, CA: Jossey-Bass.

Csikszentmihalyi, M. (2008). *Flow: The psychology of optimal experience.* New York, NY: HarperCollins.

Daloz, L. A. (1999). *Mentor: Guiding the journey of adult learners.* San Francisco, CA: Jossey-Bass.

Daloz, L. A. (2012). *Mentor: Guiding the journey of adult learners* (2nd ed.). San Francisco, CA: Jossey-Bass.

Daloz, L. A., Keen, C. H., Keen, J. P., & Parks, S. D. (1996). *Common fire: Leading lives of commitment in a complex world.* Boston, MA: Beacon Press.

Deacon, A. (2012). Creating a context of care in the online classroom. *Journal of Faculty Development, 26*(1), 5–12.

Disruption. (n.d.). In *Oxford living dictionaries.* Retrieved from https://en.oxforddictionaries.com/definition/disruption

Dixon Rayle, A., & Chung, K. (2008). Revisiting first-year college students' mattering: Social support, academic stress, and the mattering experience. *Journal of College Student Retention: Research, Theory & Practice, 9*(1), 21–37.

Dunn-Haley, K., & Zanzucchi, A. (2012). Complicity or multiplicity: Defining boundaries for graduate teaching success. *New Directions for Teaching and Learning, 2012*(131), 71–83.

Dutton, J. E. (2003). *Energize your workplace: How to create and sustain high-quality connections at work.* San Francisco, CA: Jossey-Bass.

Easter-Smith, O. (2015). Nannie Helen Burroughs: Religious leader, educator, activist. In S. Imel & G. T. Bersch (Eds.), *No small lives: Handbook of North American early women adult educators: 1925–1950* (pp. 55–64). Charlotte, NC: IAP Information Age Publishing.

Edwards, J. B., & Richards, A. (2002). Relational teaching: A view of relational teaching in social work education. *Journal of Teaching in Social Work, 22*(1–2), 33–48.

Elbow, P. (1997). High stakes and low stakes in assigning and responding to writing. *New Directions for Teaching and Learning, 1997*(69), 5–13.

Espinoza, C. (2012). Millennial values and boundaries in the classroom. *New Directions for Teaching and Learning, 2012*(131), 29–41.

Espinoza, C. (2016). *Managing the millennials: Discover the core competencies for managing today's workforce.* Hoboken, NJ: John Wiley & Sons.

Faculty-Student Relationships: University of Pittsburgh Office of the Provost. (n.d.). Retrieved from http://cfo.pitt.edu/policies/documents/Policy07-14-01web.pdf

Fletcher, J. K., & Ragins, B. R. (2007). Stone center relational cultural theory. In B. R. Ragins & K. E. Kram (Eds.), *The handbook of mentoring at work: Theory, research, and practice* (pp. 373–399). Los Angeles, CA: Sage.

Frand, J. L. (2000, September–October). The information-age mindset: Changes in students and implications for higher education. *EDUCAUSE Review*, 14–24.

Fredrickson, B. L. (2001). The role of positive emotions in positive psychology: The broaden-and-build theory of positive emotions. *American Psychologist, 56*(3), 218–226.

Freire, P. (1970). *Pedagogy of the oppressed.* New York, NY: Herter & Herter.

Frey, L. L. (2018). When it hurts to work: Organizational violations and betrayals. *New Directions for Teaching and Learning, 2018*(153), 87–98.

Garner, R. L. (2006). Humor in pedagogy: How ha-ha can lead to aha! *College Teaching, 54*(1), 177–180.

Gibson, D. M., & Myers, J. E. (2006). Perceived stress, wellness, and mattering: A profile of first-year citadel cadets. *Journal of College Student Development, 47*(6), 647–660.

Giles, D. L. (2011). Relationships always matter: Findings from a phenomenological research inquiry. *Australian Journal of Teacher Education, 36*(6), 80–91.

Goffman, E. (1959). *The presentation of self in everyday life*. New York, NY: Doubleday.

Graham, L. (2010). *What is it like to be funny? The spontaneous humor producer's subjective experience* (Electronic thesis or dissertation). Retrieved from https://etd.ohiolink.edu/

Gutiérrez y Muhs, G., Niemann, Y. F., González, C. G., & Harris, A. P. (Eds.). (2012). *Presumed incompetent: The intersections of race and class for women in academia*. Boulder, CO: University Press of Colorado.

Hayes, J. A. (2004). The inner world of the psychotherapist: A program of research on countertransference. *Psychotherapy Research, 14*(1), 21–36.

Heifetz, R. A., & Linksy, M. (2002). *Leadership on the line: Staying alive through the dangers of leading*. Boston, MA: Harvard Business School.

Hertz, J. H. (1945). *Pirke avot: Sayings of the fathers*. New York, NY: Behrman House.

Hoffman, E. M. (2014). Faculty and student relationships: Context matters. *College Teaching, 62*(1), 13–19.

Hogan, K. (2017). The academic slow lane. In M. A. Massé & N. Bauer-Maglin (Eds.), *Staging women's lives in academia: Gendered life stages in language and literature workplaces* (pp. 247–260). Albany, NY: State University of New York Press.

Holloway, E. L., & Alexandre, L. (2012). Crossing boundaries in doctoral education: Relational learning, cohort communities, and dissertation committees. *New Directions for Teaching and Learning, 2012*(131), 85–97.

hooks, b. (1994). *Teaching to transgress: Education as the practice of freedom*. New York, NY: Routledge.

hooks, b. (2000). *Where we stand: Class matters*. New York, NY: Routledge.

Hua, L. U. (2018). Slow feeling and quiet being: Women of color teaching in urgent times. *New Directions for Teaching and Learning, 2018*(153), 77–86.

Huerta, A. H., & Fishman, S. M. (2014). Marginality and mattering: Urban Latino male undergraduates in higher education. *Journal of the First-Year Experience and Students in Transition, 26*(1), 85–100.

Hurtado, S., Eagan, M. K., Tran, M. C., Newman, C. B., Chang, M. J., & Velasco, P. (2011). "We do science here": Underrepresented students' interactions with faculty in different college contexts. *Journal of Social Issues, 67*(3), 553–579.

Ibarra, H. (1999). Provisional selves: Experimenting with image and identity in professional adaptation. *Administrative Science Quarterly, 44*(4), 764–791.

Intimate. (n.d.). In *Oxford living dictionaries*. Retrieved from https://en.oxforddictionaries.com/definition/intimate

Jensen, J. M., Opland, R. A., & Ryan, A. M. (2010). Psychological contracts and counterproductive work behaviors: Employee responses to transactional and relational breach. *Journal of Business and Psychology, 25*(4), 555–568.

Johnson, K. A. (2000). *Uplifting the women and the race: The educational philosophies and social activism of Anna Julia Cooper and Nannie Helen Burroughs*. New York, NY: Routledge.

Johnson-Bailey, J. (2015). Academic incivility and bullying as a gendered and racialized phenomena. *Adult Learning, 26*(1), 42–47.

Jordan, J. V. (1989). *Relational development: Therapeutic implications of empathy and shame* (*Work in Progress* series, No. 39). Wellesley, MA: Stone Center Working Paper Series.

Jordan, J. V. (1990). *Courage in connection* (*Work in Progress* series, No. 45). Wellesley, MA: Stone Center Working Paper Series.

Jordan, J. V. (1991). Empathy and self boundaries. In J. V. Jordan, A. G. Kaplan, J. B. Miller, I. P. Stiver, & J. L. Surrey (Eds.), *Women's growth in connection: Writings from the Stone Center* (pp. 67–80). New York, NY: Guilford Press.

Jordan, J. V. (1994). *A relational perspective on self-esteem* (*Work in Progress* series, No. 70). Wellesley, MA: Stone Center Working Paper Series.

Jordan, J. V. (1997). Clarity in connection: Empathic knowing, desire, and sexuality. In J. V. Jordan (Ed.), *Women's growth in diversity: More writings from the Stone Center* (pp. 50–73). New York, NY: Guilford Press.

Jordan, J. V. (2004). Toward competence and connection. In J. V. Jordan, M. Walker, & L. M. Hartling (Eds.), *The complexity of connection: Writings from the Stone Center's Jean Baker Miller Training Institute* (pp. 11–27). New York, NY: Guilford Press.

Jordan, J. V. (2010). *Relational-cultural therapy*. Washington DC: American Psychological Association.

Jordan, J. V., & Schwartz, H. L. (2018). Radical empathy in teaching. *New Directions for Teaching and Learning, 2018*(153), 25–35.

Josselson, R. (1995). *The space between us: Exploring the dimensions of human relationships*. Thousand Oaks, CA: Sage.

Karpouza, E., & Emvalotis, A. (2018). Exploring the teacher–student relationship in graduate education: A constructivist grounded theory. *Teaching in Higher Education, 23*(6), 1–20.

Kasworm, C. E. (2008). Emotional challenges of adult learners in higher education. *New Directions for Adult and Continuing Education, 2008*(120), 27–34.

Kearney, P., Plax, T. G., Hays, E. R., & Ivey, M. J. (1991, October–November). *What students don't like about what teachers say and do*. Presented at the annual meeting of the Speech Communication Association, Atlanta, GA.

Kim, M., & Schallert, D. L. (2011). Building caring relationships between a teacher and students in a teacher preparation program word-by-word, moment-by-moment. *Teaching and Teacher Education, 27*(7), 1059–1067.

Lahtinen, A. (2008). University teachers' views on the distressing elements of pedagogical interaction. *Scandinavian Journal of Educational Research, 52*(5), 481–493.

Liang, B., Tracy, A., Kauh, T., Taylor, C., & Williams, L. M. (2006). Mentoring Asian and Euro–American college women. *Journal of Multicultural Counseling and Development, 34*(3), 143–154.

Liang, B., Tracy, A. J., Taylor, C. A., & Williams, L. M. (2002). Mentoring college-age women: A relational approach. *American Journal of Community Psychology, 30*(2), 271–288.

Lieberman, M. D. (2014). *Social: Why our brains are wired to connect*. New York, NY: Crown.

Lubrano, A. (2005). *Limbo: Blue-collar roots, white-collar dreams*. Hoboken, NJ: John Wiley & Sons.

MacKinnon-Slaney, F. (1994). The adult persistence in learning model: A roadmap to counseling services for adult learners. *Journal of Counseling and Development, 72*(1), 268–275.

MacNell, L., Driscoll, A., & Hunt, A. N. (2014). What's in a name: Exploring gender bias in student ratings of teaching. *Innovative Higher Education, 40*(4), 291–303.

Markus, H., & Nurius, P. (1986). Possible selves. *American Psychologist, 41*(9), 954–969.

Marshall, S. K., Liu, Y., Wu, A., Berzonsky, M., & Adams, G. R. (2010). Perceived mattering to parents and friends for university students: A longitudinal study. *Journal of Adolescence, 33*(3), 367–375.

Martin, R. A. (2007). *The psychology of humor: An integrative approach*. Burlington, VT: Elsevier Academic Press.

Marwick, A. E., & boyd, d. (2010). I tweet honestly, I tweet passionately: Twitter users, context collapse, and the imagined audience. *New Media & Society, 20*(1), 1–20.

Mayeroff, M. (1971). *On caring*. New York, NY: HarperPerennial.

McEwan, B. (2012). Managing boundaries in the social media classroom. *New Directions for Teaching and Learning, 2012*(131), 15–28.

McMillian-Roberts, K. D. (2014). *The impact of mutuality in doctoral students and faculty mentoring relationships* (Doctoral dissertation). Fielding Graduate University. Retrieved from https://eric.ed.gov/?id=ED567339

Merriam, S. B., & Bierema, L. L. (2014). *Adult learning: Linking theory and practice*. San Francisco, CA: Jossey-Bass.

Mezirow, J. (1978). Perspective transformation. *Adult Education, 28*(2), 100–109.

Mezirow, J., & Associates. (1990). *Fostering critical reflection in adulthood: A guide to transformative and emancipatory learning*. San Francisco, CA: Jossey-Bass.

Mezirow, J., & Associates. (2000). *Learning as transformation: Critical perspectives on a theory in progress*. San Francisco, CA: Jossey-Bass.

Miller, J. B. (1976). *Toward a new psychology of women*. Boston, MA: Beacon Press.

Miller, J. B. (1986). What do we mean by relationships? (*Work in Progress* series, No. 22). Wellesley, MA: Stone Center Working Paper Series.

Miller, J. B. (1991). Women and power. In J. Jordan, A. Kaplan, J. Miller, I. Stiver, & J. Surrey (Eds.), *Women's growth in connection: Writings from the Stone Center*. New York, NY: Guilford Press.

Miller, J. B., & Stiver, I. P. (1995). Relational images and their meanings in psychotherapy (*Work in Progress* series, No. 474). Wellesley, MA: Stone Center Working Paper Series.

Miller, J. B., & Stiver, I. P. (1997). *The healing connection: How women form relationships in therapy and in life*. Boston, MA: Beacon Press.

Murphy, R. J. (1993). *The calculus of intimacy: A teaching life*. Columbus, OH: Ohio State University Press.

Myers, J. E., & Bechtel, A. (2004). Stress, wellness, and mattering among cadets at West Point: Factors affecting a fit and healthy force. *Military Medicine, 169*(6), 475–482.

Nair, I. (2018). Joy of being a teacher. *New Directions for Teaching and Learning, 2018*(153), 45–54.

Newton, N. A., Khanna, C., & Thompson, J. (2008). Workplace failure: Mastering the last taboo. *Consulting Psychology Journal, 60*(3), 227–245.

Noddings, N. (2003). *Caring: A feminine approach to ethics and moral education* (2nd ed.). Berkeley, CA: University of California Press.

Ortiz, A. M., & Pichardo-Diaz, D. (2011). Millennial characteristics and Latino/a students. In F. A. Bonner, A. F. Marbley, & M. F. Howard-Hamilton (Eds.), *Diverse millennial students in college: Implications for faculty and student affairs* (pp. 117–133). Sterling, VA: Stylus.

Palmer, P. (1998). *The courage to teach: Exploring the inner landscape of a teacher's life*. San Francisco, CA: Jossey-Bass.

Palmer, R. T., & Maramba, D. C. (2012). Creating conditions of mattering to enhance persistence for Black men at an historically Black university. *SPECTRUM, 1*(1), 95–120.

Parks, S. D. (2005). *Leadership can be taught: A bold approach for a complex world*. Boston, MA: Harvard Business School Press.

Parks, S. D. (2011). *Big questions, worthy dreams: Mentoring emerging adults in their search for meaning, purpose and faith* (10th anniversary edition). San Francisco, CA: Jossey-Bass.

Piorkowski, J. L., & Scheurer, E. (2000). "It's the way that they talk to you": Increasing agency in basic writers through a social context of care. *Journal of Basic Writing, 19*(2), 72–92.

Pittman, C. T. (2010). Race and gender in the classroom: Experiences of women faculty of color with white male students. *Teaching Sociology, 38*(3), 183–196.

Postareff, L., & Lindblom-Ylanne, S. (2015). What triggers emotions in university teaching? *Ammattikasvatuksen aikakauskirja, 17*(2), 83–96.

Purgason, L. L., Avent, J. R., Cashwell, C. S., Jordan, M. E., & Reese, R. F. (2016). Culturally relevant advising: Applying Relational-Cultural Theory in counselor education. *Journal of Counseling and Development, 94*, 429–436.

Raven, B. H. (1992). A power/interaction model of interpersonal influence: French and Raven thirty years later. *Journal of Social Behavior and Personality, 7*(2), 217–244.

Raven, B. H. (2008). The base of power and the power/interaction model of personal influence. *Analysis of Social Issues and Public Policy, 8*(1), 1–22.

Robertson, D. L. (1996). Facilitating transformative learning: Attending to the dynamics of the educational helping relationship. *Adult Education Quarterly, 47*(1), 41–53.

Robertson, D. L. (1997). Transformative learning and transition theory: Toward developing the ability to facilitate insight. *Journal on Excellence in College Teaching, 8*(1), 105–125.

Robertson, D. L. (1999a). Professors' perspectives on their teaching: A new construct and developmental model. *Innovative Higher Education, 23*(4), 271–294.

Robertson, D. L. (1999b). Unconscious displacements in college teacher and student relationships: Conceptualizing, identifying, and managing transference. *Innovative Higher Education, 23*(3), 151–169.

Robertson, D. R. (2001a). Beyond learner-centeredness: Close encounters of the systemocentric kind. *Journal of Faculty Development, 18*(1), 7–13.

Robertson, D. R. (2001b). College teaching as an educational helping relationship. *Essays on Teaching Excellence, 13*(1).

Robertson, D. R. (2005). Generative paradox in learner-centered college teaching. *Innovative Higher Education, 29*(3), 181–194.

Rogers, C. R. (1961). *On becoming a person: A therapist's view of psychotherapy.* New York, NY: Houghton Mifflin.

Rogers-Shaw, C., & Carr-Chellman, D. (2018). *Resisting the pressures of academia: The importance of including care in doctoral study.* Presented at the Adult Education Research Conference. Retrieved from http://newprairiepress.org/aerc/2018/papers/37

Rose, E., & Adams, C. (2014). "Will I ever connect with the students?": Online teaching and the pedagogy of care. *Phenomenology and Practice, 7*(2), 5–16.

Rosenberg, M., & McCullough, B. C. (1981). Mattering: Inferred significance and mental health among adolescents. *Community and Mental Health, 2*, 163–182.

Rossiter, M. (1999). Caring and the graduate student: A phenomenological study. *Journal of Adult Development, 6*(4), 205–216.

Rousseau, D. M. (1989). Psychological and implied contracts in organizations. *Employee Responsibilities and Rights Journal, 2*(2), 121–139.

Rousseau, D. M. (1990). New hire perceptions of their own and their employer's obligations: A study of psychological contracts. *Journal of Organizational Behavior, 11*(5), 389–400.

Schlossberg, N. K. (1987). Understanding and reaching adult learners. *McGill Journal of Education, 22*(1), 9–18.

Schlossberg, N. K. (1989). Marginality and mattering: Key issues in building community. *New Directions for Student Services, 1989*(48), 5–15.

Schon, D. A. (1983). *The reflective practitioner: How professionals think in action.* New York, NY: Basic Books.

Schwartz, H. L. (2009). *Thankful learning: A grounded theory study of relational practice between master's students and professors* (Doctoral dissertation). Antioch University. Retrieved from https://etd.ohiolink.edu/pg_10?0::NO:10:P10_ACCESSION_NUM:antioch1247833338

Schwartz, H. L. (2011). From the classroom to the coffee shop: Graduate students and professors effectively navigate interpersonal boundaries. *International Journal of Teaching and Learning in Higher Education, 23*(3), 363–372.

Schwartz, H. L. (2012a). Editor's notes. In H. Schwartz (Ed.), *Interpersonal boundaries in teaching and learning* (*New Directions for Teaching and Learning* series, No. 131, pp. 1–3). San Francisco, CA: Jossey-Bass.

Schwartz, H. L. (Ed.). (2012b). *Interpersonal boundaries in teaching and learning* (*New Directions for Teaching and Learning* series, No. 131). San Francisco, CA: Jossey-Bass.

Schwartz, H. L. (2012c). Reflection and intention: Interpersonal boundaries in teaching and learning. In H. L. Schwartz (Ed.), *Interpersonal boundaries in teaching and learning* (*New Directions for Teaching and Learning* series, No. 131, pp. 99–102). San Francisco, CA: Jossey-Bass.

Schwartz, H. L. (2013). Dinner at Fitzwilly's: Intellectual mattering in developmental relationships. In N. Dominguez & Y. Gandert (Eds.), *Sixth annual mentoring conference proceedings: Impact and effectiveness of developmental relationship.* Albuquerque, NM: University of New Mexico.

Schwartz, H. L. (2017). Sometimes it's about more than the paper: Assessment as relational practice. *Journal on Excellence in College Teaching, 28*(2), 5–28.

Schwartz, H. L., & Holloway, E. L. (2012). Partners in learning: A grounded theory study of relational practice between master's students and professors. *Mentoring & Tutoring: Partnership in Learning, 20*(1), 115–133.

Schwartz, H. L., & Holloway, E. L. (2014). "I become a part of the learning process": Mentoring episodes and individualized attention in graduate education. *Mentoring & Tutoring: Partnership in Learning, 22*(1), 38–55.

Schwartz, H. L., & Holloway, E. L. (2017). Assessing graduate student work: An emotional and relational perspective. *Journal on Excellence in College Teaching, 28*(2), 29–59.

Seidel, S. B., & Tanner, K. D. (2013). "What if student revolt"—Considering student resistance: Origins, options, and opportunities for investigation. *CBE—Life Sciences Education, 12*, 586–595.

Shockley, M. E. (2013). *I'll choose which hill I'm going to die on: African American women scholar-activist in the white academy* (Doctoral dissertation). Antioch University. Retrieved from https://aura.antioch.edu/etds/42

Slater, R., Veach, P. M., & Li, Z. (2013). Recognizing and managing countertransference in the college classroom: An exploration of expert teachers' inner experiences. *Innovative Higher Education, 38*(1), 3–17.

Snyder-Duch, J. (2018). Relational advising: Acknowledging the emotional lives of academic advisors. *New Directions for Teaching and Learning, 2018*(153), 55–65.

Stanley, C. A. (2006). Coloring the academic landscape: Faculty of color breaking the silence in predominantly white colleges and universities. *American Educational Research Journal, 43*(4), 701–736.

Stebleton, M. J., Soria, K. M., & Huesman, R. L., Jr. (2014). First-generation students' sense of belonging, mental health, and use of counseling services at public research universities. *Journal of College Counseling, 17*(1), 6–20.

Steele, C. M. (2010). *Whistling Vivaldi: How stereotypes affect us and what we can do.* New York, NY: W. W. Norton.

Stern, D. (1985). *The interpersonal world of the infant.* New York, NY: Basic Books.

Strayhorn, T. L. (2012). *College students' sense of belonging: A key to educational success for all students.* New York, NY: Routledge.

Sue, D. W., & Sue, D. (2016). *Counseling the culturally diverse: Theory and practice* (7th ed.). Hoboken, NJ: Wiley & Sons.

Sugimoto, C., Hank, C., Bowman, T., & Pomerantz, J. (2015). Friend or faculty: Social networking sites, dual relationships, and context collapse in higher education. *First Monday, 20*(3). Retrieved from http://journals.uic.edu/ojs/index.php/fm/rt/printerFriendly/5387/4409

Surrey, J. L. (1985). *Self-in-relation: A theory of women's development* (*Work in Progress* series, No. 13). Wellesley, MA: Stone Center Working Paper Series.

Tobin, L. (1993). *Writing relationships: What really happens in the composition class.* Portsmouth, NH: Boynton/Cook Heinemann.

Tolman, A. O., & Kremling, J. (2017). *Why students resist learning: A practical guide for understanding and helping students.* Sterling, VA: Stylus.

Tolman, A. O., Sechler, A., & Smart, S. (2017). Defining and understanding student resistance. In A. Tolman & J. Kremling (Eds.), *Why students resist learning: A practical guide for understanding and helping students* (pp. 1–20). Sterling, VA: Stylus.

Tom, A. (1997). The deliberate relationships: A frame for talking about student–faculty relationships. *Alberta Journal of Educational Research, XLIII*(1), 3–21.

Tovar, E., Simon, M. A., & Lee, H. B. (2009). Development and validation of the college mattering inventory with diverse urban college students. *Measurement and Evaluation in Counseling and Development, 42*(3), 154–178.

Vierling-Claasen, A. (2013, January 13). *Shame and math.* Retrieved from https://prezi.com/ssrbj0xbuv4m/shame-and-math-for-jmm13/

Vitak, J. (2012). The impact of context collapse and privacy on social network site disclosures. *Journal of Broadcasting and Electronic Media, 56*(4), 451–470.

Waite, S. (2017). *Teaching queer: Radial possibilities for writing and knowing.* Pittsburgh, PA: University of Pittsburgh Press.

Walker, M. (2002a). *How therapy helps when the culture hurts* (*Work in Progress* series, No. 95). Wellesley, MA: Stone Center Working Paper Series.

Walker, M. (2002b). *Power and effectiveness: Envisioning and alternate paradigm* (*Work in Progress* series, No. 94). Wellesley, MA: Stone Center Working Paper Series.

Walker, M. (2004). How relationships heal. In M. Walker & W. B. Rosen (Eds.), *How connections heal: Stories from Relational–Cultural Therapy* (pp. 3–21). New York, NY: Guilford Press.

Walker, M., & Rosen, W. B. (2004). *How connections heal: Stories from Relational–Cultural Therapy.* New York, NY: Guilford Press.

Wanzer, M. B., Frymier, A. B., Wojtaszczyk, A. M., & Smith, T. (2006). Appropriate and inappropriate uses of humor by teachers. *Communication Education, 55*(2), 178–196.

Weimer, M. (2010). *Inspired college teaching: A career-long resource for professional growth*. San Francisco, CA: Jossey-Bass.

Weimer, M. (2013). *Learner-centered teaching: Five key changes to practice*. San Francisco, CA: Jossey-Bass.

Winnicott, D. W. (1960). The theory of the parent–infant relationship. *The International Journal of Psychoanalysis, 41*, 585–595.

Yamashita, M., & Schwartz, H. L. (2012). The coconut and the peach: Understanding, establishing, and maintaining boundaries with international students. *New Directions for Teaching and Learning, 2012*(131), 57–69.

Zell, M. C. (2010). Achieving a college education: The psychological experiences of Latina/o community college students. *Journal of Hispanic Higher Education, 9*(2), 167–186.

# ABOUT THE AUTHOR

**Harriet L. Schwartz**, PhD, is professor of psychology and counseling at Carlow University (Pittsburgh, PA), where she serves as chair of the student affairs master's degree program. Schwartz teaches a range of courses, including Social and Cultural Foundations of Counseling, Psychologies of Poverty, Foundations of Student Affairs, Career and Lifestyle Planning, Relational Practice and Leadership, Leadership and Ethics, and Adult Learning and Workplace Diversity.

In addition, Schwartz is Lead Scholar for Education as Relational Practice for the Jean Baker Miller Training Institute (JMBTI), Relational-Cultural Theory's intellectual center, founded at Wellesley College. Through her work with JBMTI, she presents at conferences and webinars, supports graduate students and other emerging scholars, and promotes the work of RCT scholar-practitioners.

Schwartz's scholarly interests include teaching as relational practice, emotion and teaching, and qualitative research methods. Her work has been published in a number of journals, including *Journal on Excellence in College Teaching, International Journal of Teaching and Learning in Higher Education*, and *Mentoring & Tutoring: Partnership in Learning*, and she has published in *SAGE Research Methods Cases* and the *Handbook of Research Methods on Diversity Management, Equality and Inclusion at Work*. In addition, she has published two *New Directions for Teaching and Learning* sourcebooks, coediting *Teaching and Emotion* (2018) and editing *Interpersonal Boundaries in Teaching and Learning* (2012).

Schwartz mentors doctoral students in qualitative research methods at Antioch University, where she earned her PhD in leadership and change. She also holds an MS in counseling and a certificate in student personnel from Springfield College. Prior to pursuing a teaching career, she worked in student affairs at Carnegie Mellon University, Bard College, and the University of Hartford.

## Creating Wicked Students

*Designing Courses for a Complex World*

Paul Hanstedt

"Hanstedt is a teacher's teacher. He approaches the college classroom with a combination of excitement, experience, skill, and humor. His goal—to create 'wicked' students, ready to face the daunting challenges of the twenty-first century—is right on point. And his strategies and recommendations are clear, practical, and instructive. I can't wait to share this highly readable and valuable book with my colleagues."—**Bret Eynon**, *Associate Provost, LaGuardia Community College (CUNY), Coauthor,* High Impact ePortfolio Practice: Catalyst for Student, Faculty, and Institutional Learning

"From its playful title to its final chapter, *Creating Wicked Students* offers a thought-provoking new approach to course design. Hanstedt guides the reader through a design process for courses where students learn skills and content and develop 'the ability to step into a complex, messy world and interact with it in thoughtful and productive ways." —**Deandra Little**, *Director, Center for the Advancement of Teaching and Learning; and Associate Professor of English, Elon University*

## Difficult Subjects

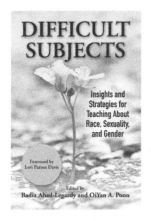

*Insights and Strategies for Teaching About Race, Sexuality, and Gender*

Edited by Badia Ahad-Legardy, OiYan A. Poon

Foreword by Lori Patton Davis

"*Difficult Subjects* offers keen insights and guidance without being prescriptive. It offers critical social analysis while being pragmatic and accessible. As educators grapple with the tensions the current administration poses, this text serves as a beautiful and necessary counterbalance as we collectively try to regain our humanity." — **Nolan Cabrera**, *Associate Professor, Center for the Study of Higher Education, University of Arizona*

"This book is a must-read for both those who are new to the classroom and those who are looking for support and sustenance to persist."— **Amanda E. Lewis,** *Professor of African-American Studies & Sociology, and Director of the Institute for Research on Race and Public Policy , University of Illinois at Chicago*

22883 Quicksilver Drive
Sterling, VA 20166-2102

Subscribe to our e-mail alerts: www.Styluspub.com